PREACHING THROUGH A STORM

PREACHING THROUGH A STORM

H. Beecher Hicks, Jr.

Foreword by William A. Jones

Ministry Resources Library

Zondervan Publishing House • Grand Rapids, MI

PREACHING THROUGH A STORM

MINISTRY RESOURCES LIBRARY is an imprint of Zondervan Publishing House, 1415 Lake Drive S.E., Grand Rapids, Michigan, 49506.

Library of Congress Cataloging in Publication Data

Hicks, H. Beecher.
    Preaching through a storm.

    Bibliography: p.
    1. Baptists—Sermons. 2. Sermons, American—Afro-American authors.
3. Pastoral theology—Baptists. 4. Hicks, H. Beecher. I. Title.
BX6452.H53   1987   252'.061   86-32538
ISBN 0-310-20091-1

Edited by Joseph Comanda
Designed by Louise Bauer

Printed in the United States of America

87   88   89   90   91   92 / EE / 10   9   8   7   6   5   4   3   2   1

To
Metropolitan Baptist Church
Through Seasons
of
Weeping and Rejoicing
Together
We Are Family

What peaceful hours I once enjoy'd
How sweet their memory still!
But they have left an aching void
The world can never fill.

God moves in a mysterious way
His wonders to perform;
He plants his footsteps in the sea
And rides upon the storm.
William Cowper

CONTENTS

FOREWORD

Rarely does a person write about his pain predicament in close time proximity to the event which produced the pain and the predicament. The normal approach is to engage in such activity long after the smoke of battle has settled, when the guns are silent and cool.

H. Beecher Hicks, Jr., has defied the norm, moved counter to custom, and dared to give a running weather report of the storm that engulfed him and his ministry for nearly five years. "Courage" is almost too weak a word to describe his latest literary piece. "Audacity," informed by honesty and candor, is perhaps the better word.

Beginning with the personal agony precipitated by the loss of his loving mother, the writer takes the reader on a nonstop journey through several storm-tossed experiences: board difficulties, attempts to muffle and muzzle the preacher, leadership challenges, false charges, character assassination, demonic assaults, the seeming absence and/or silence of ministerial colleagues, negative counsel, and a certain myopia caused by a serious attempt to view the storm on every front at one time.

When one considers that "stormy weather" of such magnitude developed and persisted in the midst of a mammoth building program, the fact that this preacher did not succumb to a spirit of bitter resignation or yield to the temptation to "throw in the towel" is indicative of guidance by Transcendant Reality. Seldom do we have the opportunity to read a sermonic pilgrimage reflecting all the dialectical forces at work in a given situation. In this work they are present in plentitude. The preacher lays bare his very soul and permits us to scrutinize him as he experiences what F. Scott Fitzgerald called "the dark night of the soul where it's always three o'clock in the morning." And then, a sunlit morning arrives on the very wings of the storm itself, giving credence to the apostle Paul's declaration, "Through much tribulation we enter the kingdom of God."

Preaching Through a Storm begins on a note that borders on fatalism. Hurt, anger, pessimism, distrust—all these are actively present, and understandably so. And the existential question implicit in the storm is this: "How does one minister to the enemies of his soul?" When a person's theological training has provided no answers, and the preacher himself describes the pastorate as "the worst job you will ever love," how does he cope with ineluctable crises?

H. Beecher Hicks, Jr., after journeying to hell and back, tells us how by showing us how. You preach through the storm, knowing even as you preach that serious preaching arouses serious conflicts. Through it all he never failed to lift up his Lord.

Ministerial heads ought to be clearer after reading such wise words of warning born out of creative and redemptive tension between the ideal and the real. In the final analysis, the One who calls us to this work, where both muck and majesty are operative, promises nothing at all except His presence.

William Augustus Jones
Bethany Baptist Church
Brooklyn, New York

PREFACE

Visions are hard to come by. Dreams rarely come true. Within the span of one's lifetime it is almost inconceivable that one can be blessed by visions and dreams and see them both come to a measure of reality. Such has been my experience over nearly a quarter of a century in the Christian pastorate. The pursuit of those realities is, in part, the essence of this work.

In a sense, the pastorate is the worst job you will ever love. Its demands are unreasonable, its calling inescapable, its machinery often unworkable, its concepts difficult to grasp, and the political realities of the work make "success" almost impossible to achieve. Oddly enough, even when those of us who are pastors come to know a measure of success (whatever that is) we must still face the undeniable truth that we did not achieve what we should have or what we could have. We always live with the uneasy knowledge that we are not, and never can be, what others think we are. The oddity of life itself is that one can achieve and pursue the elusive reality of success and never find genuine happiness or joy.

The central, underlying truth of this work is a principle well understood by those who are captured by the calling to the Christian pastorate. You never *really* learn how to pastor. The pastorate involves a lifetime of trial and failure, and only God in heaven knows the outcome. Furthermore, you can't learn this art in any class or seminar taught by the local seminary or Bible college. In the end your people are your teachers. Week by week, Sunday by Sunday, the congregation rates and grades the preacher-pastor on his witness and his work. It is a process which can be, at the same time, unnerving and gratifying.

Any lessons about the Christian pastorate which I may have learned have not come from the academic setting alone, and therefore this work proposes to have about it an air of practicality as opposed to a purely theoretical treatment of the subject. My "professors in the pews" have been far more astute than any I found in the classroom—including Mother Jackson, who called me "boy" on my first day in my first church, and the member in another church who found my sermon hour an appropriate time to read the morning paper. All of them, individually and collectively, have taught me more lessons about this profession than any textbook could contain. To them I am deeply indebted.

The reader will come to understand that this work is intensely personal. It is a reflection of those experiences and principles which have been shared with me not only by the Metropolitan Baptist Church of Washington, D.C., but shared as well by the Second Baptist Church of Mumford, New York, the Mount Ararat Baptist Church of Pittsburgh, Pennsylvania, and the Antioch Missionary Baptist Church of Christ of Houston, Texas. Each church, in its own peculiar and distinctive way, has provided both the calm and storm through which I have sought to pastor and to preach. I cannot fail to mention the church of my childhood, the Mount Olivet Baptist Church of Columbus, Ohio, where my father, Dr. H. Beecher Hicks, Sr., served as pastor for thirty-three years. It was the Mount Olivet Church that shaped and molded my perceptions of the meaning and mission of the church, and it was my father who taught, almost imperceptibly, those lessons on preaching and storm endurance which would serve me well in days and years to come.

The author is grateful to many persons within the Metropolitan family who offered comments and suggestions as this work was in process. I am grateful as well to my friend and brother in the gospel, Dr. Granville A. Seward of the Mount Zion Baptist Church of Newark, New Jersey, for his theological counsel and editorial advice.

PREFACE

I acknowledge with a deep sense of thanksgiving the untiring work of Mrs. Dorothy L. W. Smith, my faithful administrative assistant, for countless hours spent on sermon reproduction, and the generous and gracious assistance of Ms. Jacqueline Gray, whose word-processing skills contributed invaluably to the generation of the manuscript.

It should be acknowledged at the outset that sermons are never purely original. They are the product of our experience and of lessons taught by others. I do not know how many fellow-preachers or authors have contributed to my knowledge bank and thus influenced the frame or the content of sermons I have preached. If I have infringed upon them in any way, I offer my gratitude as well as my apology. In this connection, it should be noted that sermons—including the ones in this book are not at their best when reduced to print. The setting and the tone of worship, as well as countless inflections and intonations, control the ebb and flow of the preaching moment. Sermons were never intended to be read. They must be seen, felt, heard, and experienced.

I cannot emphasize too greatly that the sermons are necessarily the product of the black preaching idiom in which the language is often more poetic than concise. In preaching one is allowed wordiness which is not permitted in those documents prepared for the reading public. One may also discover a kind of repetitiveness and a lack of variation in approach. All of us are creatures of habit. As I have come to understand it, the storm-tossed preacher will often resort to the monotony of routine and the safety of a highly predictable preaching pattern. This was certainly the case in my own preaching experience. While I recognize these faults, I have chosen to expose these sermons, nevertheless, in the hope that they may clearly identify many of the pitfalls to be avoided by others in the preaching moment in general and preaching through a storm in particular.

George Washington Carver once suggested that "a common thing done uncommonly well will command the attention of the world." If what we achieve in the Christian pastorate does come to the attention of the world, it is frightening indeed. Sometimes success is more fearful than mediocrity or failure. One lives daily with the fear that it is possible to be a failure at being a success. Yet we are not speaking here to the issue of success or failure—they are illusive commodities at best. We are speaking of the loving relationship which can exist between pastor and people and of one pastor's willingness to say, "Please be patient with me. God is not through with me yet!"

H. Beecher Hicks, Jr.
Washington, D.C.

INTRODUCTION

A light rain had fallen the night before, washing clean the air of this midwestern American city, leaving it cool and crisp on this particular Sunday. I was the guest preacher for an anniversary service of a thriving, growing congregation pastored by one of my dearest friends in the ministry. I had shared with this congregation before, and I anticipated a warm reception and uplifting worship.

I was not mistaken. The sanctuary was filled to capacity. Music from the one-hundred-voice choir thundered with the majesty of classical Christian hymnody and with the unmistakable beat of contemporary gospel music performed tastefully and without flaw. The worship was marked by applause, laughter, tears, and shouts of praise.

Then, in the midst of that glorious time of worship, it happened. My mind, unbidden, raced eastward to the congregation God had given me to shepherd, and I was overwhelmed by the contrast. I had come to preach for a congregation bathed in such unmistakable joy, leaving behind a congregation immersed in incredible sorrow. All the dreams I had nurtured for my own people were flashing on the panoramic screen of another setting. Before me sat a people nourished and thriving on the Word, excited about the church, moving forward now in their new sanctuary, well-ordered, disciplined, and happy. I could not say the same for my own.

It hurt. Intensely. To the core. To the quick. The hurt was indeed so painful that tears streamed down my face. My host, sensing my hurt, placed a gentle hand on my knee and assured me, "He is able!"

I did not know then what I know now: I was a preacher caught in a raging, violent storm—a storm so fierce in its intensity that it threatened my sense of well-being, my sense of self-esteem, my sense of spiritual balance. As I view it now, my very life hung in the balance.

I was caught in that storm for three years as pastor of one of the largest black Baptist congregations in America. At first the turbulence centered around the church's decision to replace a century-old structure with a new edifice for our Christ, but it spread until it encompassed the whole congregation. It left in its wake the unavoidable debris of accusation, misunderstood motives, threats, violations of Christian principles, the abandonment of traditional Baptist discipline, and a people—although not irretrievably split—confused, uncertain, and groping for light in the swirling seas of doubting blackness. Worst of all, I considered it my fault.

Through it all I held on to two beliefs that I still hold to this day: that God had called me to preach and that in a strange but significant manner He had called me to be the pastor of this people. But I was perplexed. If my calling was genuine, then why this confusion, why this struggle, why this storm? To pastor, to shepherd the flock of God is difficult at best. To do so under a cloud of conflict and controversy makes the task seemingly impossible to achieve.

There is within the mindset of many black preachers a prevailing notion that if a man is able to preach, he can overcome most any difficulty. Our people, so the logic runs, are rooted and grounded in the preaching event, and no matter how deep the difficulty, no matter how serious the schism, a pastor can survive it through the power of God as made manifest through the preached Word. My experience of three years' duration was to put that theory seriously to the test.

Hence this book attempts to examine the place and the purpose of preaching within the pastoral setting and to discover whether, indeed, one can preach through a storm.

I know from personal experience that the storm definitely affects the preaching engagement. Many advised me in the midst of the storm to go to the pulpit and "simply preach

Jesus!" Others encouraged me to keep the message upbeat and positive. Easier said than done, my friend! It is no simple matter for a preacher caught in the throes of a storm to remain objective and fair.

The storm provides an unnatural, alien, even hostile environment in which preaching with power becomes nearly impossible. There are rare moments when the reverse is true—when the conflict provides grist for the mill, so to speak, and when the challenge brings out the best in the preacher. More often than not, however, the preacher is prone to want to "fight back," to make a pulpit response to the forces working against him. In so doing he loses both a measure of his integrity as a preacher and the preaching perspective required of a pastor.

There are many sides to any story and, admittedly, the pulpit should not be used to tell only one. Even so, the preacher must remain faithful to the gospel as he understands it and as it is revealed to him. There is often a word of truth which is positive in its nature, but because of the distorted perception of the pew will be heard in its negative connotations. There are applications of the Scripture which do not and are not designed to make people comfortable. They are designed to "reprove, rebuke, and exhort" and must not be compromised. The gospel is a two-edged sword. It not only cuts going in and coming out, it cuts the one who wields the sword as well as the one toward whom its thrusts are projected.

The preacher must always be willing to examine his motivation and remain sensitive to the psychological power of the sermon. And he should seek to be positive. But he must never flinch from declaring revealed truth either. Clearly, however, to will and to do are vastly different things.

This is not just another book on how to preach good sermons. Nor is it an attempt on the part of the author to display what he believes to be significant sermonic wares. (While these sermons are not my "best"—if there are any "best"—they do represent a faithful sampling of my sermonic struggles during a three-year period of my pastorate.) This book is born out of a conviction that there is power in preaching and that preaching must not only be kissed by divine urgency, but subject to critical analysis, psychological investigation, theological testing, and biblical examination as the preacher himself stands and speaks under the awesome and awful scrutiny of eternity.

Additionally, this book serves other important purposes. For one thing, it should send a message to pastors caught in storms that, however regrettable, their situations are not unique. There is a storm raging in churches across the nation. It has become a daily occurrence to read in the newspapers of preachers who for one reason or another are being capsized in their theological boats by the storms of the church. In fact, if the reader of this work is a pastor, we may reasonably assume that he is, in the words of William Augustus Jones of Bethany Baptist Church in Brooklyn, New York, either "coming out of a storm, in a storm, or heading for a storm."

The problem is broad and pervasive. No church is immune from the storm of struggle, controversy, and division. In a book entitled *The Gathering Storm in the Churches*, Jeffrey K. Hadden analyzes the storm of the church primarily from the point of view of white, Protestant churches struggling with the problem of integration and the new wave of social activism in the sixties. His analysis could apply equally well to the contemporary black church. The problems are far different, but the work of the storm is the same:

> In recent years, three crises have been emerging in the Protestant churches: a crisis over its very meaning and purpose for being, a crisis of belief, and a crisis of authority. These three crises are obviously interrelated. Clergy have challenged the traditional role of the church in society because they have reinterpreted the theological basis of their faith and in so doing have come to feel that their faith involves a much more vital commitment to the problems of this world. Laity have challenged the authority of clergy because they do not share their under-standing of the meaning and purpose of the church. The shattering of traditional doctrines has weakened the authority of the clergy, for it is no longer certain that they hold the keys to the kingdom.[1]

INTRODUCTION

The book is designed to speak a word not only to veteran pastors, but to the young novitiates of the craft. Unfortunately, modern seminaries are not training young theologs in the art of tension reduction and conflict resolution within the contemporary church. The church is already in a state of crisis with regard to the number of young men and women who are committing themselves to the Christian ministry. Too many alert and agile young black minds are being enticed by the lucrative positions offered by corporate America. We should not also frighten them away with threats of congregational insurrections. This book is meant to be descriptive of the real world "out there" and to assure aspiring pastors that, while the storm is real, there is a way to preach through it.

The book is also meant to provide laypersons with an understanding of pastoral leadership. Strange as this may seem, a preacher cannot survive a storm apart from the patient and supportive presence and action of the people he serves. Perhaps through this work laypersons may also come to understand better the storms in which they have unwittingly participated and become themselves agents of storm reduction in their own congregations.

Finally this work speaks directly to the congregation which I have served now for nearly ten years. I trust it may help them understand better the pastor as a person and give them an appreciation for the peril and pain of preaching through a storm.

I have not wanted this to be a self-pitying or self-absorbed account. Nor has my purpose been to be vengeful, vindictive, spiteful, or judgmental. For that reason, I have steadfastly omitted names of persons who have been involved in my own personal storm within the pastorate. Wherever conflict is out of control within the Christian community, the judgment is corporate—it rests upon both pastor and people.

"Those who cannot remember the past are condemned to repeat it." This work had to be written, then, so that we might, to paraphrase Terence, draw from others the lesson that may profit ourselves.

I'VE BEEN IN THE STORM SO LONG

PROLOGUE

When caught in the midst of a storm, a minute will seem an hour, an hour will seem an eternity. Time perception is lost; life and death hang on every moment. Such a thought, no doubt, caused our foreparents to sing, "I been in the storm so long!"

At the "ripe old age" of forty-four years, it is clearly inaccurate, if not impertinent, to suggest that one has been in the storm "so long." Yet my impression is valid if for no other reason than the fact that it seemed "so long" (would it ever end?) to me. Every day seems endless in a storm; every night knows no termination to the depth of its darkness. Patience is a word that loses its meaning—indeed, it appears ludicrous in the face of the urgency one feels. One cannot see "the light at the end of the tunnel." One doubts the tunnel has an end. It is not helpful to hear, "Good things come to those who wait." Waiting seems no more than hopeless inertia. It is wasted counsel to advise a storm-tossed seaman, "It's always darkest before the dawn" or "If you can just hold out till tomorrow, everything will be all right." The dawn seems to bear its own darkness, and it seems futile to "hold out" while groping in the dark for something or someone by which one may simply "hold on." In the time of my own discontent, the winter of 1981, I was already learning to sing, "I been in the storm so long!"

Actually, it all started with an honest-to-goodness thunderstorm. In the summer of 1977, on my birthdate, the Metropolitan Baptist Church voted by overwhelming majority to call me as its fifth pastor in more than a century of Christian service. At the time of the call, I was pastor of a large, historic congregation in Houston, Texas. The two churches had much in common: an old structure, significant historical heritage, an older membership marked by the unmistakable absence of many babies in the Sunday morning nursery.

Given such similarities, one could question—if but for a moment—the wisdom of God in ordaining and directing (demanding?) what seemed at the time to be a lateral movement of ministry. I should have known. God does, indeed, "move in mysterious ways." On the night of my call to this significant pulpit in the nation's capital, the event was ushered in on the wings of a storm. I am told that the old structure shook with the vibrations of thunder and lightning, as more than a thousand members crowded the sanctuary to cast their ballot. And while the storm raged, the first ballot was cast. Its verdict was clear: our family would move northward to begin a new ministry. Could it be that the storm that June night in 1977 was both sign and symbol of storms which were yet to come?

Those first years of the pastorate were distinguished only by the predictable rising and falling of the usual tides of church life. The "honeymoon" lasted far longer than normal; it appeared that we were afloat on a calm and placid lake.

The first of those storms to come was my own. The ground was covered with snow as the clear, crisp air of a January night settled into stillness. I picked up the receiver on the first ring of the phone and heard the words, "Mama has just taken her flight." In the middle of the night it was the dawn of death. My mother had gone home to be with God, and my own private, personal, internal storm began to rage.

I had never known death. I had counseled others in their experience of the anguish of death. I had stood by the bedside of countless others who, in the words of Deacon Matthew Carter, had "changed worlds and swapped lives." I had studied clinically the meaning of death, including having read

Elisabeth Kübler-Ross's *On Death and Dying.* But I had never really known in a personal way the assault, the insult, the indignity of death.

The death of my mother was not a tragedy; it was a sweet release from pain and suffering for her. For me, however, it was in a very real sense a personal catastrophe. Death in this instance required of my psyche adjustments I was not prepared to make, calling forth emotions with which I had never had to deal. The support of family, friends, and church did not ease the pain or assuage the grief. I could not make sense of these strange and unwelcome feelings which intruded into the seeming balance of my life.

I recognized the classic symptoms. Nonacceptance. This is not really happening. Not to me. Not now. Guilt. What could I have done that I did not do? Why was I absent from home at the moment of her flight? Why did I permit my brother to be the only child of my parents to stand along with my father in this hour of family need? Depression. I must not be a very good person, a very good son. What else is going to happen? This is not the end. . . . There is more to follow. . . . Why am I so lonely in the company of so many friends? With whom am I angry—God, family, medical science, myself? I have become Jeremiah in my own time—my head is waters, my eyes a fountain of tears, I weep day and night (Jeremiah 9:1). For me, there is no balm in Gilead, there is no physician there (Jeremiah 8:22). Nobody knows the trouble I see . . . I been in the storm so long!

In the context of personal pain and suffering, I had to preach in a storm—my own storm. I remained away from my pulpit for two Sundays, but I soon had to return to the real world and minister to those who were similarly suffering. What would I say? What *could* I say? The hours had become "tedious and tasteless." I had no enthusiasm, no fire, no apparent power for preaching.

Months later, feeling the almost imperceptible pressure of subtle reversals in the church program in general and sensing my own personal inability to deal with my own destiny and date with death, I needed to share my feelings, I needed to communicate my hurt, and I wanted to pronounce the benediction on my pain. I sought to share it with my people in an attempt to "preach it out." I found myself, in a moment of rising grief, struggling to preach in a storm.

Sermon: HOW LONG THE NIGHT?

Weeping may endure for a night, but joy cometh in the morning (Psalm 30:5).

Permit me to share a word with you that is marked by a measure of personal pathos and pain. I am caught on the proverbial "horns of a dilemma," for this is a sermon I do not want to preach. Were the choice mine alone, I would close this Book and pronounce the benediction.

There is, however, at work in my spiritual mind, a force which cannot be denied and a word which will have its way. If never before, I am this morning a man preaching under the twin agony of compulsion and conviction. While I would not burden you with this matter of personal searching and internal testimony, I assure you I have no choice in this matter.

I must also confess that what I have to say today is not new. There is nothing novel in the offering of this hour. There is no attempt either veiled or obvious to put some new twist on this ancient text. Indeed, your familiarity with the substance of this sermon—because you have read this word so often and because it is a part of your spiritual and biblical con-sciousness—provides at least a common ground of under-standing and even perhaps a point of unified departure.

All of this, by way of introduction, is to suggest that I want to look again at this word of the psalmist David. "Weeping may endure for a night, but joy cometh in the morning."

This is a word of whispering hope that shouts its confidence. It is the testimony of a man who knows what it is to be in sorrow's valley and who has himself lingered in the very "shadow of death." This is the valedictory of one who has been stained by the indelible ink of sin and now is able to rejoice that his sin has been forgiven and his iniquity pardoned.

David is one who, perhaps more than others, is entitled to this exuberant chronicle of confidence. He has been in battle with a bear. He has, in place of the armies of Israel, been placed in combat with the giant called Goliath. This one who so skillfully and deftly handled the harp in the court of King Saul was a benefactor of intense loyalty and, at the same time, the target of intense hate. The lyrics of this psalm could only be sung by one who had countless enemies, but who still had a Friend; by one who had already been to hell a hundred times, but who still had a hope for heaven; by one who deserved the anger of God, but who had come to know the sure mercies of the Eternal.

I suppose that's the reason why this word has always been lifted up as the ultimate declaration of hope in hopeless situations. That's the reason it is often produced as the panacea for man's ills. It is the ultimate answer to perplexing questions and lingering doubts. "Weeping may endure for a night, but joy cometh in the morning."

And I want to believe that, I genuinely want to believe that. I believe your presence today is indicative of your desire to believe that tears are temporary and that joy is the only permanent reality. I genuinely want to be personally persuaded that "the flowers of character are watered by the tears of tribulation." But I have a question. A serious question. If weeping endures for a night, I want to know, "How long the night?"

*　　*　　*

I remember as a child that quite often the family would climb in the car to go on a trip. Very often we made the journey from Ohio to Louisiana, an excursion of more than one thousand miles. But just as soon as the car rounded the first corner, somebody would ask the question, "Daddy, when do we get there?" And I suppose that's the reason I need to ask this question. David says that the morning is coming, but I want to know when do we get there? Maybe if I knew how long I had to wait, it would help me make it through the night.

I don't know how you find it, but the older I get, it seems like my night lasts longer and longer, and I'd like to know the time parameters for this night in which I'm living. Maybe these are sunshine days for you, but there's a curtain of midnight which has draped itself around my soul; and even though I look the same and act the same, there's been a drastic change in my outlook on life. Maybe if I had an idea how long this night would last I'd have some realistic hope for looking for a light at the end of the tunnel. I'd like to know, "How long the night?"

Six centuries before Christ, Isaiah in his prophecy was heard to raise the question in similar terms, "Watchman, what of the night?" (Isaiah 21:11). In other words, watchman, you're at your appointed post of duty. We're down inside the city, and you have the vantage point of standing on the lofty precipice of the city's fortified wall. You've got a view of the danger. You're at the proper point to warn us if some enemy lurking in the darkness will bring danger and destruction to our city. The preacher is God's watchman. So tell us, watchman. Warn us, watchman. Alert us, watchman. "Watchman, what of the night?"

It is a terrible thing when you ask the watchman and he doesn't know. It's a terrible thing when you go to the fountain of faith and the fountain is dry. What a tragedy to go down to the church and say, "Preacher, have you heard any word from the Lord?" And he says, "I don't know." It's a terrible plight to ask direction from your guide and your guide is lost. Isaiah said, "Watchman, what of the night?" To which came the response, "The morning cometh, and also the night" (Isaiah 21:12). In other words, I don't know what's happening. I have a hope for a new morning, but I'm living and languishing in the inescapable reality of the night. That's why I wanted to inquire, "How long the night?"

I just want to know how long this night is going to last. How long this night of mute misery and speechless sorrow and inescapable hurt? How long this night of briny tears which never seem to dry up? How long this night of deepening depression when there appears no relief in sight? How long this night when I must lie on the lonely pillow of my own thoughts on the bed of unbelievable agony and distress? How long this night when I can't tell my closest friend what I feel and almost dare not tell myself? How long this night when the things I've given my life to are shattered and broken and I no longer have the will to stoop down and fix them with worn-out tools? How long this night when the vision God has given me appears trampled on by those who see but do not see and hear but not the voice of the Eternal?

How long this night? Henry Wadsworth Longfellow said, in "A Psalm of Life,"

> Tell me not, in mournful numbers,
> Life is but an empty dream!
> For the soul is dead that slumbers,
> And things are not what they seem.

How long this night? Was Shakespeare right? Have "all our yesterdays . . . lighted fools the way to dusty death"? Is life "but a walking shadow, a poor player that struts and frets his hour upon the stage and then is heard no more"? Is it really "a tale told by an idiot, full of sound and fury, signifying nothing"?[1]

How long this night? Is Job right? "Man that is born of a woman is of few days and full of trouble." Is Ecclesiastes right? "Vanity of vanities, saith the Preacher, vanity of vanities; all is vanity."

How long this night? I know David said weeping would endure for a night, but I still want to know how long is this night?

*   *   *

It ought to be said parenthetically here that perhaps you won't think my question so innocuous and nonsensical when I remind you that it is night. We are living in a social night, in a time when the social fabric and fiber of the land is being ripped apart by special interest groups and perverted politics, a time when the economics of this insanity is presided over by bigger and better bigots who no longer keep children out of school—they just starve them to death once they get in.

We're living in a social night when the meaning of poverty is being redefined daily. There was a time if you made ten thousand dollars a year, you were somebody. Now if you make ten thousand dollars a year, it's shame on you! It's night.

We're living in a moral night. A night which has seen the line between right and wrong erased. A moral night. A night which says marriage is a thing of the past and home is where your hat is. A moral night. A night which says that the end of life is to get high by any and every means available. A moral night. A night when traditional values are gone, children are telling their parents what to do, and parents are afraid of the children they feed and clothe. Don't look now, but it's night!

Some of us are involved in personal nights. Some of us may be afflicted by what Søren Kierkegaard calls "the sickness unto death." Somebody here has some sickness in the house. Somebody here went to the doctor last week, and the news was not good news. Somebody here just got out of the hospital, and you know you're on your way back. Somebody here has a secret you haven't told anybody because it is night.

Additionally, it is night spiritually. The deepest night in my soul is when I realize that church is not church like it used to be. There's something strange and unsettling in church when folk would rather applaud than say amen. There's something spiritually wrong when church organizations spend more time planning picnics and parties than they do praying in prayer meeting. There's something spiritually wrong when folk want to sit three hours in a style show, but can't sit thirty minutes through a sermon. It's night. Socially, morally, personally, spiritually, it's night, and I just want to ask, "How long the night?"

*   *   *

Because I'm so curious about this matter, I began to give thought to the night factor in religion. I had not thought of it before, but the story of the Bible hangs on the hinges of some strange and unusual occurrences which took place in the night. That leads me to suggest that maybe God does some of His best teaching through encounters in the night. I looked again at the Nineteenth Psalm, and there I heard David declare, "The heavens declare the glory of God; and the firmament sheweth his handiwork. Day unto day uttereth speech, and night unto night sheweth knowledge." Maybe there is some knowledge to be gained in the night that I can't learn in the sunshine. Maybe there are some lessons God has to teach at a midnight hour that you can't absorb in the brilliance of the noonday sun. The Book says:

Jacob wrestled with the Angel, in the night.

God sent the death angel to Egypt, in the night.

Israel was led through the wilderness with a cloud by day and a pillar of fire, in the night.

Belshazzar saw a finger writing, MENE, MENE, TEKEL, UPHARSIN on his palace wall, in the night.

Jesus was born with the angels singing, "Glory to God in the highest." They were singing in the night.

The disciples went fishing and caught nothing, in the night.

Nicodemus came to hold a conference with Jesus, in the night.

Jesus spoke to the waves and told them, "Peace, be still," in the night.

There was a prayer meeting in Philippi when Paul started to pray and Silas started to sing and the jailhouse started to rock, in the night.

Judas betrayed Jesus in an old upper room, and the Gospel says when Judas went out it was night.

Jesus prayed in the Garden of Gethsemane, "Father, if it be possible, let this cup pass from me." He prayed it in the night.

Jesus hung on the cross on Friday, and even though the clock of time said three in the afternoon, the clock of eternity said it was midnight. They tell me the sun refused to shine, and when "the sun don't shine," it's night.

How long the night? The standard mode of understanding this night predicament is to look to the testimony of others. No matter how hard it is with you, no matter how dismal your days or how miserable your nights, somebody else has been where you're going. That's why we like to hear others testify about what the Lord has done for them.

We like to hear David say, "He that dwelleth in the secret place of the most High shall abide under the shadow of the Almighty. . . . Thou shalt not be afraid for the terror by night; nor for the arrow that flieth by day" (Psalm 91:1, 5).

We love to hear Jeremiah say, "His compassions fail not. They are new every morning; great is thy faithfulness" (Lamentations 3:22–23). We don't mind joining with Job who looked forward, and I believe he could see it, to when the morning stars would sing together and the sons of God would shout for joy. It makes us feel mighty good when we read over and over, "Weeping may endure for a night, but joy cometh in the morning."

*   *   *

I've been waiting on joy a long time, however, and I am not so sure that the testimony of others is sufficient. I don't know how long your night was (or is), but I do want to know how long my night will be. It sounds strange for a preacher to ask, but I want to know how long is my night?

I know there's a better day a coming, but how long is the night?

I know one day every day will be Sunday and every month the month of May, but how long is the night?

I know "God moves in mysterious ways His wonders to perform," but how long is the night?

I know "all things work together for good for those who love the Lord," but how long is the night?

I know I need to "wait on the Lord and be of good courage," but how long is this night?

I know "Jesus is near to comfort and cheer just when I need Him most," but how long is my night?

I know that "earth has no sorrow that heaven cannot heal," but how long is my night?

I know "He knows just how much we can bear," but how long is my night?

I know "there's a bright side somewhere," but I still need to know how long the night!

I'm learning that the longer my night, the less time I have to wait. You can't run through the night, you can't skip over the night, you can't avoid the night. You've got to endure the night. The Word says "He that endureth to the end shall be saved." If you want to know how long the night, it's not long. The same God who closes the curtain of the night also opens the curtain of the morning.

How long? Not long! He promised to wipe every tear from my eye.

How long? Not long! In fact, it will be "soon one morning when this life is o'er, I'll fly away."

How long? Not long! He promised a city with "a tree of life for the healing of the nations. There'll be no more sorrow, no more sadness, no more sighing, no more dying, and no night there."

Good night, sorrow!

Good night, sadness!

Good night, sickness!

Good night, pain!

Good night, heartache!

Good night, death!

"Weeping may endure for a night, but joy cometh in the morning."

EPILOGUE

I didn't make it. It was a valiant effort, but I didn't make it. It was soul-bearing, it was a public confessional, but as I look upon it now, I didn't make it. For those who shared the moment (stunned, sitting in silence while this preacher sobbed and cried his way through three-fourths of the message, with no shred of understanding of what was going on), this was not the gospel they had come to expect, not the good news of life in Jesus Christ. It was real, authentic, and genuine in its purpose and intent, but the sermon did not define the storm, it did not lessen the storm or provide the needed psychological tools with which the hearer or the preacher could survive the storm or make it through the night.

No doubt some folks went down the aisle after the doxology and the benediction muttering, "Don't tell me your troubles, I've got troubles of my own."

Surely this is not the way we are to preach through a storm. Or is it?

In retrospect, there are some lessons the preacher may learn from this experience of seeking to preach through a storm.

First, the preacher is not exempt from personal crisis. Some black preachers live in such a surrealistic world of power, pomp, and pageantry that not only do the people not expect of them the experience of personal crisis, but tragically, they come not to expect it of themselves. Must the preacher-pastor always be a tower of strength? Must the preacher-pastor always be an automaton not programmed for pain? Must he always be the example of faith without doubt, all answers and no questions? Certainly not! Preachers and parishioners must come to acknowledge, to confess, and to deal forthrightly with the essence of their creatureliness. In a word, even preachers are entitled to be human. We have every right to hurt and to be given the liberty to express all the human emotions of pain, anguish, anger, love, and human need. Such expression is a right of humanity which need not be abdicated and must not be abrogated.

At yet another level, the pastor who seeks to preach through a storm need not expect that those to whom he preaches will understand, be empathetic, or in any way be affected by his personal crises. Such an expectation is not within the pale of reason, primarily because those who are the residents of our pews are caught in their own personal storms which seem to be of far greater import (at least to them) than our own. They come to the worship experience reeling from the effects of their own turbulent winds, and to some extent they feel that the preacher has no right to compound their problems with his own. Their attitude is, "If your storm and my storm are the same storm, it may be acceptable to share your thoughts, for they are a reflection of my own experience. If, on the other hand, your storm is not expressive of mine, I came to have my problems solved, my questions answered, my wounds healed. Deal with your own storm on someone else's time."

If, then, we must acknowledge our humanity and if, at the same time, we must not invade the space of others with our own personal concerns, to whom shall we turn? The answer to the question is as simple as the Word we preach. The storm of hurt and loss and death requires a reliance on the deepest resources of our faith. This is the moment of ministry "when deep calls to deep" and when the lessons we seek to teach others must be applied to our own lives.

The question is, can the congregation be prepared to be supportive and understanding of the pastor's humanity, grief, personal conflict, and faith crises? If the pastor-preacher has allowed his humanity to be obvious, the congregation has an empathetic springboard from which to respond. However, if the pastor-preacher has been emotionally separate and distant, the sudden change which reveals his human side will find the congregation unprepared to deal sensitively with it.

In one of the last moments I spent with my mother as she lay in University Hospital, I joined with her in reciting the Twenty-third Psalm. Cancer had riddled her body relentlessly, and from time to time her cognition of time, place, and personalities around her wavered. There was something, however, which never left her—a reliance on the sure mercies of God and the unfailing faithfulness of the Father. I just looked at the Twenty-third Psalm again, and this is what it says, "Yea, though I walk *through* the valley of the shadow of death, I will fear no evil." Death: we never "get over" death, but we can get *through* it. We can go through it to the green pastures of a satisfied spirit and a wholesome understanding of the eternal purposes of God for our lives. We can preach through a storm and, in the end, our "cup runneth over."

I recently visited again the Greenlawn Cemetery where we tenderly placed my mother to rest. I noticed on this visit a sign at the entrance which read: NO OUTLET. The sign is a mistake. It is grossly inaccurate for the child of God. For some the cemetery seems to be the end; it is the final chapter, the grave is all there is. But I am confident that there is, for those who claim the Eternal in their lives, an outlet. I am sure of it, for He has promised it. One day we shall meet those whom we now miss and we shall see Him face to face.

> Hide me, O my Saviour, hide,
> Till the storms of life be past;
> Safe into the haven guide,
> O receive my soul at last!
> *Charles Wesley*

PREDICTING A STORM

PROLOGUE

Any responsible meteorologist will tell you that predicting a storm is a tricky business. With all the advances of technology and the science of weather forecasting, tomorrow's weather report is still just an "educated guess." Nevertheless, the effort is worthwhile. The price to be paid for ignoring the signs of a coming storm in loss to both property and person can be catastrophic indeed. To pretend that the storm is an unavoidable circumstance which defies precaution can result in untold suffering and perhaps death. Experienced sailors of the sea have learned to respect the signs of nature. One adage advises, "Red sky at night, sailors delight. Red sky at dawning, sailors take warning."

Similarly, the preacher-pastor who would survive the storms of the ministry must become adept at the art of storm prediction. This does not mean that the preacher-pastor must be constantly looking for trouble, always searching for a rumor to squelch, and suspicious of a storm at every wisp of the wind. It does mean, however, that with proper diagnostic (and even detective) devices the pastor-preacher may be forewarned of the brewing disturbance, warn others of its potential impact, and while saving others, save himself as well. While it may be theologically and ethically irresponsible to counsel, "Any port in a storm," it would be tragic indeed to see the storm clouds gather and be unable through ignorance or unwilling through apathy to take the necessary steps to ensure safety and protect the life of one's ministry.

Make no mistake about it, storms do have their value. It is precisely because we go through storms that we learn the lessons of survival. Were there no storms, the boats of our lives would rock on in the monotonous waves of sameness. Threatened with a storm, some are tempted to label it as a mistake on the part of either God, the pastor, or the congregation. Richard Bach, however, in his book *The Bridge Across Forever,* suggests that

> There are no mistakes. The events we bring upon ourselves, no matter how unpleasant, are necessary in order to learn what we need to learn; whatever steps we take, they're necessary to reach the places we've chosen to go.[1]

In the unfolding drama of my own storm experience, there were several clear and unmistakable signs of its coming.

The first sign of my storm was *a disruption of the board process.*

The longer I stay in the pastorate the more I become convinced that church boards are for pastors both blessing and cursing. They are a blessing because it is important for any pastor to be surrounded by God-fearing and God-guided laypersons who are committed to the redemptive causes of the kingdom and who clearly see themselves in the role of assistants to the pastor as he seeks to fulfill the role of undershepherd and to "equip the saints for the work of the ministry." They are a curse because boards often attract those seeking power for themselves who are bent on objecting to and rejecting any and all pastoral proposals or congregational directives.

For the first four years of my pastorate, I found the board process to be as productive as it might be in any Baptist church. Then without warning, influential board members who had previously been models of responsible leadership suddenly and inexplicably turned hostile and uncooperative. It was the first sign of trouble to come.

Despite these storm clouds, the congregation moved steadfastly toward a predetermined date for construction. Loan documents and commitments had been secured, the board had been authorized to proceed with legal implementation, funds for the edifice were coming in at a rate unprecedented in the church's history. All seemed well.

More storm signs accumulated.

The second sign was *an attack on the church's fiscal integrity.* A special offering fund disappeared mysteriously, and it was whispered about that someone in a pivotal position of leadership was culpable. An investigation failed to produce any serious implication of guilt, but an ominous wind was blowing. Through it all, things proceeded on schedule. We had the ground-breaking ceremony in April of 1981, followed by a lavish ground-breaking banquet. A national dignitary spoke. The city council passed a laudatory resolution. All seemed well.

The clouds began to darken. By midyear, the second financial plan for the building project had been rejected by the board. Some opposition board members, seeking to undermine the church's credibility in the financial community, made unauthorized calls and visits to lending institutions. The power and influence of a minority of key board members became more readily apparent. After negotiations and attempts at reconciliation, the board recommended and the church approved a delay in the construction process until a more substantial sum for the project had been secured. It was now clear that all was not well.

More clouds appeared.

The third sign of the storm was *an all-out attack on the organizational structure of the congregation.* A number of concerned members began calling for major revisions to the church's constitution. They advocated redefining the role and responsibility of the pastor and creating new supervisory committees.

The storm clouds began to gather. Besides the internal opposition, the church now also had to contend with outside forces. The community was enraged that we intended to demolish a structure built by former slaves. A hearing was called by the Committee on Historic Preservation and Landmarks to determine if the church had the right to make its own decisions about its own property. The hearing room resembled the annual meeting of the Hatfields and the McCoys, with antagonists on opposite sides of the room. After more delay, the decision finally came: the church was not a landmark—it bore no historic or architectural significance which was not typical of church construction during the period. What a tragedy! A decision about the very existence of the church was made by persons outside the fellowship, people uninterested in its mission or its Christ and more than a little amused by the internal bickering of the "saints." The *Washington Post* had a field day.

In the midst of the storm I preached. "How to Silence a Preacher" was first preached at the installation of one of my sons in the ministry who had been called to serve a church of similar historic moment and age in the New England corridor. The sermon was subsequently revised for presentation to an assembly of ministers convened from across the nation for the Progressive National Baptist Convention, Inc.

The signs of the storm had been difficult to detect at first, but now that they were apparent, it seemed clear that the opposition was directed against my leadership and my authority as preacher-pastor. The storm clouds were saying emphatically, "Preacher, shut your mouth!"

Sermon: HOW TO SILENCE A PREACHER; or, Shut Your Mouth!

When they were by the house of Micah, they knew the voice of the young man the Levite: and they turned in thither, and said unto him, Who brought thee hither? and what makest thou in this place? and what hast thou here? And he said unto them, Thus and thus dealeth Micah with me, and hath hired me, and I am his priest. . . .

And they said unto him, Hold thy peace, lay thine hand upon thy mouth, and go with us, and be to us a father and a priest: is it better for thee to be a priest unto the house of one man, or that thou be a priest unto a tribe and a family in Israel? (Judges 18:3—4, 19 KJV).

38

> Keep quiet, put your hand upon your mouth, and come with us
> (Judges 18:19 RSV).

It was only a few days ago, during a return to the place of my theological sojourn, that I picked up a work entitled *Postscript to Preaching*.[2] In Dr. Gene E. Bartlett's latest writing, he raises a question regarding the importance of the ministry of proclamation. As one preacher speaking to another, he asks if perhaps contemporary preaching has become dull and repetitious and if, in the process, preachers have themselves become slovenly and careless. He goes further to question if perhaps modern preaching tends to glorify the preacher far more than it glorifies God. Moreover, he wonders if the claims for preaching are not simply proud illusions and if the hope of having a ministry in which preaching is central is not a futile one in our secular times. At the very least, says Bartlett, we need to reexamine the nature of the preaching encounter and to ask whether its claims are still valid in our secular day.

I suppose it was because I have read and heard so many similar inquiries that I did not take this author's words with any sense of abiding seriousness. It was only when I picked up Carnegie Calian's work entitled *Today's Pastor in Tomorrow's World*[3] that I began to view with alarm this business of preaching and preachers. It alarmed me because, even though the book jacket advertised that the author would call us "back to basics," his new book about the new pastor did not contain one chapter clearly devoted to the priority of preaching. That led me to the inescapable conclusion that perhaps Bartlett was right when he suggested that preaching and preachers need to be reexamined to determine if our claims are still valid for our times.

Quite naturally, these literary offerings have occasioned in my mind some questions of my own. If preaching is no longer what it used to be or what it ought to be, if preaching can no longer be posited as a priority for the "faith once delivered to the saints," if preaching is no longer popular, what has been designed to take the place of preaching? In an era when our culture has become chaotic, in an era when our morals have become comatose, in a day when our churches are weakened by a kind of spiritual anemia and our pews are filled with a new strain of hypnotized hypocrites, in a day when our politics have become perverted and our government seems to be living in the twilight zone of ethical anesthesia, I'd be interested to find out whatever happened to preaching? In a time when our philosophers, our thinkers, our scientists, our ethicists are confounded and confused, tossed to and fro on every fresh wind of doubt, I want to know what has become of God's man? Where is he who is able to speak that word heard while listening in the midnight watches with the Eternal? I just think we ought to ask who is responsible for negating and abdicating the divine-human dialogue called preaching? In a day when too many of our theological schools are producing pathetic products of quasi-intellectualism, I'm curious to know who's preparing to preach and who's planning to be an advocate of the Almighty.

This matter is of critical importance for those of us who claim prophetic status in the Christian church and for those whose spiritual groundings have come from the seedbed of blackness. Search for the root of black religion, and you will find preaching. Search for the sustaining factor of the black church, and you will discover preaching. Search for a starting point for a meaningful ministry, and you must inevitably begin and conclude with preaching.

It is abundantly clear that black people are a people of the Word. We are by nature, I fear, a preaching-oriented people. We come from a preaching tradition. Preaching sustained and nurtured us during days of slavery. Preaching gave us hope in those "days when hope unborn had died." Preaching is the focal point of the black religious experience today. Behind every black institution of education and higher learning is a preacher preaching. Behind the beginnings of our oldest insurance companies, financial institutions, and benevolent societies started for blacks by blacks is a black preacher preaching. Behind the most significant social revolution of the twentieth century was a black preacher preaching.

Is it not natural, then, that when you tell me that

preaching may be limping on its last leg, when you tell me that preaching has become a proud illusion and a futile hope—is it not reasonable that somebody ought to inquire, "Whatever happened to preaching?"

*   *   *

These questions about preaching and preachers keep haunting the hallways of my mind because, as I read this Book, preaching used to have a place of prominence and importance which evidently it no longer enjoys. I am under the impression that preaching was important. John the Baptist came preaching and teaching in the wilderness of Judea. Mark says that when the Christian movement began, "Jesus came . . . preaching" (Mark 1:14).

Peter preached with such power that three thousand souls joined the church at one time.

When Peter joined up with John, their message was so menacing, their preaching was so powerful, that the prevailing political order provided a reservation gratis at the local city jail.

Paul established his theology of the doctrine of salvation on the principle of preaching. Paul asked the question, did he not?

> How then shall they call on him in whom they have not believed? and how shall they believe in him of whom they have not heard? and how shall they hear without a preacher? And how shall they preach, except they be sent? as it is written, How beautiful are the feet of them that preach the gospel of peace, and bring glad tidings of good things! (Romans 10:14–15).

God thought preaching was important. Did not Paul say, "It pleased God by the foolishness of preaching to save them that believe" (1 Corinthians 1:21)? God thought preaching was so important, in fact, that even though He had only one Son, He made Him a preacher!

I don't mind telling you that I'm strangely moved, I'm disturbed and distressed, for it appears that something has happened to preachers. I don't know why. It just seems we're not really producing many princes of the pulpit. It disturbs me that we don't have any Elijahs who have opened up a school for prophets. It is a source of my continued agony that the voices that used to be heard are now hushed on the other side of eternity and there seem so few to take their places. It unsettles me to know that when men ask Zedekiah's question, "Is there any word from the LORD?" (Jeremiah 37:17), all we hear is the insulting sound of silence. And so, I want to know, who silenced the preachers? Who told the preachers to hush? Evidently somewhere, somehow, sometime, somebody said, "Preacher, shut your mouth!"

This matter of silent preachers bothered me so that I began to read in the seventh book of the Septuagint, commonly known as the Book of Judges. There in the unfolding drama of Israel's life comes a moment which points poignantly to the preacher predicament. The children of Israel had made their way to the land of promise. Each of the tribes had been assigned land for their living. Only the tribe of Dan was yet without a homeland. In their determination to secure an adequate domicile they sent out a committee—five men of valor. Now, as they were on their way to spy out the land of Laish, they spent the night one hundred miles to the south, somewhere near Mount Ephraim. While there they discovered a young man named Jonathan who was serving as a priest in the house of Micah.

That was the moment when the property committee became the pulpit committee. They went back to the children of Dan with a glowing report that the land they had chosen was fit for their dwelling. It was a land of prosperity and abundance. But they also declared, "While we were gone, we also found a young preacher. He has all the appropriate instruments for the altar, and he has the necessary training and academic credentials we specified in our job description. He has everything that we need, and we ought to put him to use in our service."

This word is a strange word. It says that while the tribe of Dan was on the way to its new home, they stopped to have a conversation with the young Reverend Doctor Jonathan. When they arrived, they didn't ask Jonathan if he wanted to serve as their preacher. They simply took his robes and all his paraphernalia, and before he could say a word, they said, "Keep quiet, put your hand upon your mouth, and come with us." In other words, "Preacher, shut your mouth!"

And so, if you don't mind, I just want to spend a moment or two with you to analyze this matter of silencing a preacher. I thought it might be of importance to you to understand the dynamics of a situation that might cause someone to tell the preacher, "Shut your mouth!" I assure you that I want to approach this matter with a sensitive and sympathetic spirit. For every preacher wants to have a church. The preacher without a church is like a farmer without a field. And there was Jonathan, serving as the resident priest in the house of Micah.

It ought to be said, parenthetically, that there's something perverse about the assignment to be a hired hand, to be "one man's preacher." But in this case I believe I can understand the dilemma. Jonathan was a preacher who had something to say but nobody to say it to. And that's why the pulpit committee had a convincing argument when they said to him, "Wouldn't it be better for you to come and preach for a tribe than to preach for one man?"

*   *   *

The preacher ought to be careful when in search of a crowd for whom to preach. Sometimes I get nervous and uneasy around crowds. It's difficult to distinguish between where a crowd ends and where a mob begins. You do remember that it was out on Calvary that they had a crowd that crucified Jesus!

Having a crowd in your church means only that you have the *potential* for worship. Not every crowd that gathers up is the same as a "waiting congregation." Not every group of folk that join on a corner on Sunday morning have come hungering and thirsting for the Word of God. Your concern ought to be not how many are present, but how many are praying! When I stand up to declare God's Holy Word I want a praying church. I've got enough pew-sitting, bench-warming, sideline specta- tors. I want somebody out there who knows the worth of prayer and does not mind calling up heaven.

No matter how badly you may want a church, before you go to your next assignment you'd better be sure the Lord has called you and the Lord has sent you. Just as sure as you move to a church because it appears to be a greater opportunity, more people, more money, I can assure you it also has more mess and more hell-raisers than you can shake a stick at!

Anytime the pulpit committee swells your head talking about how big you're going to be because of how big they used to be, anytime folk "call" you because of what they've got rather than because of the ministry they hope to share, anytime folk start out talking about a big house and big cars and big money, you can be sure that's the same thing as saying, "Keep quiet, put your hand upon your mouth, and come with us." In other words, "Shut your mouth!"

*　　*　　*

Quite honestly, I find it hard to handle this shut-your-mouth business. But as I think about it, there are several elements at work, busily engaged in the business of silencing the preacher.

The first thing that seeks to silence the preacher is the prevailing socio-political and economic climate of America. The record of history will reveal that the driving force in the achievement of racial justice and social advancement has been the black preacher. The birthplace of the current wave of liberation movements in America has been the black church. We need to understand that black preachers have brought about more change in America than all its courts could adjudicate and all its congressmen could legislate.

When you see America's insistence on maintaining alli- ances with repressive governments, when you see America's clandestine relationship with the racist regime of South Africa, when you see the conservative bent of the current government which takes pleasure in the instruments of war and in the ability to amass the missiles of annihilation, it ought to tell you something. Our national leadership has openly espoused "A Time of New Beginning," which for black folk means a time of sudden ending.

This "new beginning" is based on the faulty assumption that America will be stronger by cutting out the lifeline of its people. We've been told that things will be better by cutting back on taxes, cutting back on spending, and cutting back on regulations. What it means is that black folk will have fewer jobs than they now have and very soon they will have no social security as well. The logic is that if the base of power for the preacher is the church and if the base of the church's power is in its people, then cut out the jobs, cut out the money, cut out food stamps, cut school lunches, cut educational loans, cut out the medical care, and not only will you destroy the only independent institution in the black community, but at the same time America will be saying to preachers, "Shut your mouth!"

What I say may sound farfetched, but I, for one, think that we've been asleep on this matter of energy in America. We need to understand that in every revolution the transportation of the troops is vital. If you can't move, you then become subject to all manner of ambush and sneak attacks. And so now gasoline is high, and it will get higher. The trains have disappeared from their tracks, and air fares are now as high as the planes in which we fly. Don't look now, but blacks are being confined to their urban reservations in the name of an energy crisis, and just as soon as we're caught and confined you'll hear somebody say, "Shut your mouth!"

We need to wake up to the reality that if America can push Cubans out the back door and let Haitians go to their death in American waters and at the same time maintain an iniquitous relationship which supplies to Israel the technology and the aircraft to bomb exiled Palestinians, with whom black people have a genetic relationship, what chance do you have in your little church by the gas station? There's something tragically wrong with a nation which spends more energy exterminating a Mediterranean fruit fly than it does the rats and roaches which infest and infect our people every day.

The reason the society at large wants to silence the preacher may well be because the preacher is under orders to speak a word about morality. The preacher is under orders to preach to the issues of institutional iniquity, governmental greed, personal perversion, and societal sin. Nobody wants to hear the preacher say, "Righteousness exalteth a nation: but sin is a reproach to any people." Nobody wants to hear the preacher say, "The wages of sin is death; but the gift of God is eternal life." The culture wants a preacher it can control. The culture does not want a preacher of power. It wants a preacher who will be victimized by his own vacillation, compromised by his own compromises; they want a willy-nilly, foot-pattin' head-scratchin', chicken-eatin' preacher whose ethics will always be in conflict with his appetite, just so they can tell him, "Preacher, shut your mouth!"

*   *   *

There is yet another method by which the society seeks to shut the mouth of the preacher. I assure you I do not mean to be offensive, but necessity is laid upon me to tell you that whenever the preacher's moral life is called into question, he has just lost his voice. In recent days, the most damaging indictment of the preacher is not in the arena of traditional moral indiscretion, but in the arena of homosexuality. "Coming out of the closet" is the vogue of our culture and, indeed, the black church has not escaped the advent of those whose sexual and personal identity has been confused and misdirected. Homosexuals are literally perching on pews, playing our pianos, and even peering over our pulpits.

The church's position on deviant behavior in general and homosexuality in particular has never been imprecise. Biblically and morally the black church has always seen such behavior as abhorrent and unacceptable. Homosexuality is the only sin that God gave up on:

> Wherefore *God also gave them up* to uncleanness through the lusts of their own hearts, to dishonour their own bodies between themselves. . . . For this cause God gave them up unto vile affections: for even their women did change the natural into that which is against nature: And likewise also the men, leaving the natural use of the woman, burned in their lust one toward another; men with men working that which is unseemly, and receiving in themselves that recompense of their error which was meet (Romans 1:24, 26–27).

Moreover, homosexuality is not simply a matter of the ethnic, but a matter of the ethical. When black men were ripped and raped from African soil, I suggest that those who survived the "middle passage" would not have made suitable candidates for a gay liberation movement. Black males have historically stood as a symbol of male sexual superiority to white males. Myths related to the black male's sexual capacity, appetite, and endurance stereotyped him as a macho among machos.

The attempt to emasculate, neuter, and castrate the black male is sufficiently recorded in the annals of America's history. One might well conclude that the growing numbers of black male homosexuals has more to do with the deliberate castration of the black male image by a degenerate democracy than it has to do with personal sexual preference or the influence of hormones or heredity. To destroy a culture, to destroy a people, all one need do is to destroy in its leaders the capacity for spinal erection and incapacitate any sense of ethical ejaculation. To destroy the so-called black male myth, the white American society encourages our men to spill their seed in an unproductive and unregenerative void. Those who bear within their bodies the sacred seed of untold generations are literally casting their pearls before swine. Regrettably, black preachers, both male and female, are not exempt from this scathing word of judgment.

These comments are critical, for they have to do with the preservation of life as opposed to the celebration of death. The growth of the homosexual population in the black church is epidemic and therefore frightening. The black church has failed to speak this word to our men and has spawned a generation where things act like men and men act like things. The black church *is* affected by the developments of the larger culture, and although conservative black churchmen have not burned homosexuals like Salem witches, it is nevertheless true that their involvement and influence in the black church is not so much the result of biblical grace as it is of suffering tolerance.

This is not to suggest that homosexuals have no place in or should be banned from our churches, but it is to say that the work of redemption and reclamation must be part and parcel of the priorities of the prophetic, lest we die a moral death more devastating than the physical. The implication is clear that as long as our moral pants are down, the world will be heard to say, "Preacher, shut your mouth!"

* * *

There is yet another matter which clearly can serve to infect us with a chronic case of prophetic laryngitis. It is an issue which has the potential and power of dividing us from ourselves, against ourselves. It is the issue of women in the ministry. Now, my brothers, we must walk carefully here, for there is within us a reservoir of self-righteous rebellion and sanctimonious theological trappings which must be dealt with openly and honestly. I don't mind confessing that I've had great personal agony and trauma in wrestling with this matter, but like it or not, the issue is clearly before us. And just as there are two sides to every issue, so it is in this situation.

Women need to understand what may be happening in the context of our society. It is historically clear that the leadership in the black community has traditionally been vested in the hands of the black preacher, and it is also clear that the majority of black preachers has been, and continues to be, male.

While I do not believe that conservative religionists are so naïve as to believe that women would be less vocal spokespersons than men, I do believe they are shrewd enough to believe that the issue itself can lead to our own division and destruction, effectively shutting our mouths.

There might also be room for the argument that the causes of liberation which white women are seeking might not necessarily be appropriate causes for black women. White male preachers have never been accused of lifting a prophetic voice, so at the very least there exists the possibility that white female preachers might reverse that trend.

Black women have always been liberated in areas that were not open to black males. And it is abidingly true that the pulpit has been the only place of free expression and leadership for black males in America, historically and in a contemporary sense. Even female preachers will admit that the Bible does not necessarily or specifically aid their cause. Attempts at biblical proof-texting fall far short of the mark, and a search for scriptural support in this matter ranges from tenuous to nonexistent. There is no escaping the fact that Jesus chose as his disciples twelve men. The question is whether that choice was a matter of sex or a matter of tradition.

In the spirit of equal rights, however, the other side of the coin must also be seen. We might as well face the unassailable reality that the black church population is three-quarters female. Not only do black women comprise the predominant church population, they are responsible, through their consistent stewardship, for the expanding base of everything from beliefs to budgets. Stated negatively but precisely, the black male minister who agrees to pastor an all-male black congregation is either an incurable optimist or a hopeless fool.

I must also tell you that as I have made my way to the seminaries of this country, there is a growing population of female students who are alert, intelligent, and serious about their calling. We must face the fact that female preachers are not on the way, they are here! And if blame must be placed, then it must be situated squarely upon male shoulders. We have not encouraged, we have not trained, we have not taught our young men to make themselves available to be used by God. We need to encourage our young people to be lawyers and doctors, but somewhere in the process we have forgotten to tell them of the highest of all callings.

Don't ever forget that there are more vacant churches in America today than there are men in seminaries to fill them. The truth of the matter is that God never leaves Himself without a witness (Acts 14:17); it doesn't say "a male witness," or "a female witness," but "a witness." I may not know what the answer is, but I do know that if God can't find enough men, if God can't find enough women, if these refuse to speak, even the rocks will cry out.

My only cause is to beg that we not be so divided over the issue of sexuality that we neglect the matter of spirituality. If we wind up divided hopelessly over this issue, we may be guilty of a form of bigotry more vicious than Jim Crow and more biting than Bull Connor's dogs. If we permit ourselves to be divided over this issue—which, incidentally, will not assure us entrance into the kingdom—you may be sure the world is ready to declare, "Preacher, shut your mouth!"

*   *   *

The group that wants to silence the preacher in a most profound sense in some instances is the church group. The people who really want the preacher to shut up are those who sit in the pews. They don't come right out and say such a thing crudely and commonly. They have too much class, too much training and upbringing. But they have subtle ways of saying it to you. What they do is, they say to you: "Now, Reverend, we don't want you to worry about the church. Don't worry about the money. And don't give a thought about the trustees. You just preach on Sunday and leave the church to us." And when you hear that, it means "Shut your mouth!"

It is indisputably true, however, that God put only one person in charge of the church. The Book says, "And I will give you pastors. . . ." Not boards, pastors; not committees, pastors; not nosy sisters who try to run everything in the church from the bedroom to the board room. "And I will give you pastors according to mine heart, which shall feed you with knowledge and understanding" (Jeremiah 3:15).

That church group has another not so subtle way of

silencing the pastor when they put the clock on him. "Now, Brother Pastor, you're a fine man and I just love you so much, but one thing—you just preach so long." Church folk will stay out all night long and never look at their watches, but just wait until twelve o'clock on Sunday! The preacher had better get it straight right early that quantity is not synonymous with quality, but neither is brevity synonymous with salvation. My folk know I'm through when I'm through when I'm through! You might also know that if they can shut your mouth, that means they intend to open theirs.

*   *   *

I cannot in good conscience conclude without telling you there is yet another manner church folk have of silencing the preacher. If they can't shut your mouth theologically or socially or ethically, they'll shut it economically. Folk get mad with the preacher and then won't put any money in the church. Now that'll make you hush in a hurry! Don't you know it's not the preacher's money, it's God's money? You can try to hold back the preacher's cash if you want to, but you're "messin' with your blessin'."

The Book says:

> Bring ye all the tithes into the storehouse, that there may be meat in mine house, and prove me now herewith, saith the LORD of hosts, if I will not open you the windows of heaven, and pour you out a blessing, that there shall not be room enough to receive it (Malachi 3:10).

The Book says, "Touch not mine anointed, and do my prophets no harm" (Psalm 105:15). You can hold back your money if you want to, but you'll be messin' with your blessin'.

Don't let anybody tell you to shut your mouth. The world has never wanted a preacher who didn't mind preaching. Peter and John preached so one day that they wound up in prison. The magistrate told them, "We strictly forbade you from preaching in this name." But I heard those preachers say, "You don't understand. We ought to obey God rather than man."

Somebody's trying to tell you to shut your mouth. The only thing I can tell you is the same thing Paul told Timothy, "Preach the word. Be instant in season and out of season." Don't let anybody shut your mouth.

> I'll tell of the Savior,
> I'll tell of His favor,
> I'll tell it wherever I go.

EPILOGUE

"Shut Your Mouth!" as a sermonic exercise had consider-able impact. It was not, nor was it intended to be, an exhaustive treatment of the negative influences at work against the preacher-pastor, but it did serve notice that the preacher would be on guard, at least aware of the presence of the storm and the implications of its blowing.

Preaching under the best of circumstances and conditions is a difficult and awesome task. The objective of preaching must not be to preach a great sermon, but to preach a faithful sermon. The importance of a sermon is not, in the words of Dr. Gene E. Bartlett, information, but germination; not what it achieves, but what it sets in motion. The sermon must be judged not only by the manner in which it is expressed, but to whom it is addressed; and it must be addressed not simply to a particular person, but to an experience as well. Even in this moment of reflection I am not certain what this particular word achieved, but I am certain that it was a word that could not be ignored.

I am aware that it may be difficult for the casual reader to understand the depth or the scope of the storm which I am describing. The cursory description which I have given may indeed occasion more questions than provide answers. For those of us who were a part of this difficult scenario, it may appear that the half has not been told. Suffice to say, however, that this experience of conflict and controversy was extremely divisive and destructive to the higher purposes and calling of the church. To expose these details of conflict is neither "linen washing" nor "bloodletting." It is, rather, an examination of those *events*, as opposed to persons, which brought a measure of jeopardy to the credibility of the church of which we were and are a part.

The matter of predicting a storm is also essentially related to the preaching process. The preacher is the agent of good (God's) will. His integrity and credibility are questioned whenever, through conflict, he loses the power of persuasiveness as a communicator. Pastor and people are persons whose lives are at stake and who, because of their imperfections, reflect at every level the nature of their humanity. The ability and the imperative to communicate must never be compromised.

At base, preaching is designed to make a difference in the lives of persons. God is concerned about the moral hygiene of society, and He is equally concerned about the spiritual hygiene of the church as the body of Christ. If we are to make this difference in persons and in community, if we are to be agents of change, we must clarify our relationship to the culture and to ourselves. Even through preaching, the church comes to examine itself as it stands in the light of the demands of the gospel.

If the reader detects in this sermon a hint of anger, the perception is accurate. I am of the opinion that one need not be ashamed of or apologetic for righteous indignation at obvious assaults upon one's integrity and motives. The congregation has a right to know and the preacher has a responsibility to communicate that such assaults will not be blithely accommodated. This is not to suggest that the pulpit should be used as a platform for confrontation. Quite the contrary. But the pulpit is the only platform of prophetic power available to the preacher. He must use it in wisdom, but he ignores it to his detriment and demise.

My anger in this instance had another source as well. I felt betrayed by the deficiency of my own theological training, and I deeply resented that it had not prepared me for this crisis in my ministry.

The church is done a disservice when seminaries presume

that theology and biblical studies alone çan prepare the graduating theolog to face the storm that is raging in the churches. It is essential that they also receive training in the areas of administration and management, as well as the ill-defined and neglected area of church politics. To do less is to continue to send crippled preachers to the pastorate, their doom sealed by inevitable storms.

Do not underestimate the pervasive power of the storm. Its effect can be devastating to mind and body. During this onslaught my physical stamina waned, and I found myself hospitalized with a dangerous case of high blood pressure. As I look back upon it, I may have been trying, unconsciously at least, to escape the fray. I do not bring this matter to your attention to evoke your sympathy. It is significant because it had identifiable symptoms and because it nearly made me the unwitting sacrificial lamb offered up on the altar of the storm.

The preacher-pastor must jealously guard his psychological and physical well-being, lest he become a casualty of the storm and be silenced for eternity. Preaching through a storm requires of us vigilance in body, mind, soul, and spirit. It is in this way we love our Lord best.

MAINTAINING RELATIONSHIPS

PROLOGUE

It is all too easy in the midst of conflict to lose perspective, to see only the negative, to overlook whatever positive elements there may be in the situation. Yet even in a storm, a pastor can draw comfort from a good relationship with the faithful people in his congregation.

The pastor-preacher is related to his people in numerous ways. In an extremely large parish (memberships over one thousand), maintaining those relationships is especially critical and requires continuous care and attention. These relationships which surround the pastor-preacher are pivotal in that they form the visible (and often invisible) network of support which is able to blunt the fierce effects of pastoral storms.

The people I have been privileged to pastor are, on the whole, kind, loving, supportive, and loyal to both pastor and church. I must confess that I was not fully able to appreciate or acknowledge that in the midst of the storm. It is clear that during the years of our most trying experiences together we were influenced and affected by a small but vocal minority. Indeed, the force of that influence is still to be felt and seen. Experience has taught us that storms do not die in a day—the sting of the wet, whipping winds of internal strife is yet to be felt.

But within this congregation are people who are serious students of the Word, talented laypersons who untiringly work for the progressive movement of the church, committed

Christians who practice by word and deed the lessons taught, and stewards of their resources, tithers on the order few pastors will see in a lifetime of preaching. The church to which God has called and sent me is, by any standard of comparison, a great church.

A pastor cannot impose that kind of loyalty and faithfulness on a congregation. It must be earned over time, and it must be maintained. In fact, one is not so much named pastor or called to be pastor as one comes to claim the authority of the pastorate through time and testing, time often punctuated by the presence of storms. That is especially true today.

In the past, the primacy and authority of the pastor-preacher in the black church was unquestioned, but I have seen that change during my two decades of service. In my congregations I have observed legitimate efforts by members to participate in the leadership of the church evolve into attempts to strip the office of preacher-pastor of the authority and power that belong to it both historically and biblically.

I have treated in an earlier volume, *Images of the Black Preacher: The Man Nobody Knows*,[1] the various leadership styles of the black preacher and how they are perceived, both positively and negatively. Let me say here that I have noticed three elements in the makeup of contemporary black congregations that have led to challenges to the traditional authority of the pastor-preacher. Two of them are recent developments, and the third is an old phenomenon that has had renewed popularity in our time.

First, today's congregations are better educated. The preacher is no longer the most highly educated person. Second, related to it, today's congregations have within them persons knowledgeable about and skilled in the use of management systems. Third, today's congregations have within them people who seek power in the church to compensate for their inability to exercise it in their places of employment.

To take a balanced view, however, I believe that there is an equal number of people within the black church community who require and expect strong leadership from the pastor-preacher. The preacher who does not work diligently to establish a strong leadership base will forever be caught in a storm occasioned by the ambiguity of divided leadership and authority. Clearly, the pastor must be the pastor in its most positive and productive meaning. Primarily because anything multi-headed takes on monstrous qualities, it is of critical importance that the pastor not be intimidated into abdicating his role as undershepherd to the flock of God, the overseer of the covenant community, the primary person (parson) in whom Christ invested the leadership of the church He established.

Threats to pastoral authority can also have positive aspects. The storms which rise in the preacher-pastor's life have the effect of removing the tendency toward unjustified arrogance. Because the preacher, despite the arguments given above, remains the most powerful and influential person within the congregational life, he is sometimes tempted "to think more highly of himself than he ought"—arrogance, plain and simple. The attention, the accolades, the gifts all serve in some measure to convince us of our own importance. A positive contribution of the storm is its ability to keep us humble. One preacher of memory suggested that the opposition forces within his church were actually his "quality control department." With regard to finances, my father is fond of saying that black folk have a running prayer of agreement with the Lord: "Lord, if you'll keep him humble, we'll surely keep him poor!"

When caught in a storm, then, it is important and appropriate to ask, "What is my purpose? What am I really trying to achieve with God's people?" Are we as pastors guilty of an iniquitous arrogance to presume that because we say it, it ought to be done—without question, without reservation? If we are honest with ourselves, we will have to admit that there are times when the answer to the foregoing questions may well be yes. Such storms can have positive value if they serve to "depedestalize" the preacher and keep him humble.

Sometimes the storm that threatens a pastor's leadership may arise principally because the pastor has failed to communicate a vision with enough clarity to ignite the minds and the hearts of the people he seeks to lead. Norman Cousins, in his work *Human Options*, reminds us that

> Ideals do not become translated into working reality just because they are needed. They have to ignite in men's minds. They have to develop explosive force. They have to blast their way through mountains of resistance, tradition, and orthodoxy.[2]

A pastor must work at maintaining his relationships with his people and at imparting the vision the Lord has given him for them.

Among the many relationships a pastor-preacher is involved in, three stand out for special mention: his relationship with his own family, with the saints of God in the congregation, and with the congregation as a whole.

Family

Primary to the pastoral sense of well-being and security is the maintenance of the family relationship. Many preachers (and I include myself) are often guilty of gross neglect of family. The barber never gets a haircut, the cobbler has holes in his shoes, and very often the preacher-pastor gives little attention to those closest to him who need his care and concern, and whose concern and care he also needs. The apostle Paul counseled preachers about the care of their souls (the essence of their being), warning that it is possible for a preacher to become so involved in saving others that he fails to save himself and, indeed, those nearest to him. Dr. Gene E. Bartlett, in his book entitled *The Audacity of Preaching*, has raised this issue:

> Is the family a source of renewal for the minister in his work? As any sound family relationship is a renewal for those in it, so the pastor's family must help to restore perspective and the understanding so essential to his ministry. There is nothing like a family to build a man up or to cut him down to size, according to his need—absolutely nothing![3]

Indelibly etched in my memory is a cold winter morning when the storm surrounding me was particularly acute. I had been criticized, attacked, and accused. My integrity had been questioned at every imaginable point. As I viewed it, my entire future in the ministry was in jeopardy. On that morning of my discontent, my three children—Henry, Ivan, and two-year-old Kristin—came in while I dressed for church, bearing a gift with a card that simply said, "Cheer up! Everything's going to clear up!" Humbly, I shed tears of joy and thanksgiving.

Through it all, my wife Elizabeth never murmured or complained. Indeed, I am confident that at the height of an extensive letter-writing campaign, Liz received numerous uncomplimentary letters and phone calls which she has never shown to me or even discussed with me—a loving attempt to shield me from these additional gusts of the storm. In so doing, she and the children became victims of the storm as well. I am grateful to God, as any preacher must be, for this kind of family relationship, which must be jealously guarded and maintained.

Saints in the Household of God

Not all members of the church are saints. All are striving to become, presumably, but they have not as yet arrived. I am convinced, however, that in every church there are some legitimate "saints" or "angels," if you will, whom God places near the heart of the preacher-pastor. The church which I have been called to serve has more than its share of these sainted personages. They are the ones who, through every gale or storm, stand by the chosen pastoral leader. Very often—it is a sign of their humility—their work goes unnoticed. They often show their support in small, inconspicuous ways—sometimes as little as a warm smile, an extended handshake or "holy hug," a card or letter by mail, or a phone call "just to say I'm praying for you."

It is a relationship which, through the loud roar of the storm, cannot be heard by the human ear. It is loud enough to be heard, however, in those dark nights of agony of the soul. To nurture such a relationship is not to prefer some over others, but it is to acknowledge that the promises of heaven are sure: "He will send angels to bear you up lest you dash your foot against a stone." For them, the preaching moment is of particular significance as they continually need a word from their pastor to assure them that their support is needed, that their concern and caring are acknowledged, that he will provide for them a word of whispering hope, and above all, that their contribution to the ministry is appreciated and respected. Every preacher in a storm must thank heaven for the saints in the household of God.

The Congregation

The ministry of pastor and people is based on a relationship which began on the first day he climbed the stairs of the pulpit. At some point, especially in congregational churches, the membership judged that they would invest in him the power and prerogative of the pastoral office. That loving confidence must never be forgotten or taken for granted.

The maintenance of a sound and principled relationship with one's congregation requires both thoughtfulness and prayer. During the course of our struggle to maintain a wholesome atmosphere within our congregation, the church adopted as its theme the slogan "We Are Family!" and at every point of our church life some effort was made to accentuate this theme. I normally consider theme-selection for church years a rather artificial mechanism. In this instance, however, it served to confirm in our minds the unity of purpose and spirit which would be required for our very survival as the people of God.

The biblical concept of the "family of God" must be illumined in any storm-conflict within the church, lest the components of the body live by the mistaken notion that they can exist apart from the other organisms or indeed apart from the whole. Programming should reflect this "family-of-God" orientation and center around community building rather than conflict resolution.

It seems ironic to say this, but the maintenance of a wholesome pastor-people relationship is critical in a storm.

Often, in the heat of the storm, 80 to 90 percent of the membership will either be unconcerned about the fray or will have consciously or unconsciously decided that their personal storms are of far greater importance. They will continue to present themselves in the house of worship asking, "Is there any word from the Lord?" By and large, they resent the conflict and the confusion and look continuously to the man of God for a word which will give them leadership in their lostness and light in a time of darkness. They want to get on with the business of being and becoming the church and with dealing with those issues both temporal and spiritual which greet them at the critical crossroads of their lives.

It is an awesome task—this business of reconciling, consoling, assuring, guiding, guarding, and loving—to which the pastor is called and committed. Every person in our pews is involved in his or her own season of distress and grief. There is no peace in their world, on their jobs, in their homes. There must at least be peace in the church. The preacher-pastor must take seriously his role as peacemaker. Jesus said it best: "Blessed are the peacemakers: for they shall be called the children of God" (Matthew 5:9).

Sermon: IN PURSUIT OF PEACE

John's shoes are very often uncomfortable. And when shoes don't fit, they hurt you to your soul. But the Cobbler from Calvary says, "Wear the shoes anyhow."

I want to lift a word which is to be found in Paul's letter to the Ephesians. It is in the second chapter of that pivotal work in the Pauline corpus, verses 10–14.

> For we are his workmanship, created in Christ Jesus unto good works, which God hath before ordained that we should walk in them. Wherefore remember, that ye being in time past Gentiles in the flesh, who are called Uncircumcision by that which is called the Circumcision in the flesh made by hands; That at that time ye were without Christ, being aliens from the commonwealth of Israel, and strangers from the covenants of promise, having no hope, and without God in the world:

But now in Christ Jesus, ye who sometimes were far off are made nigh by the blood of Christ. For he is our peace, who hath made both one, and hath broken down the middle wall of partition between us.

There is none among us who does not at some deep, personal, intimate level long for the reality of peace. I would remind you that the absence of war and conflict do not constitute the presence of peace.

Peace—real peace—is an internal phenomenon.

Peace—real peace—enables you to sleep when the wind is howling.

Peace—real peace—assures you of the right even when standing in the presence of wrong.

Peace—real peace—lets you see yourself standing when all around you are falling.

Everyone at an intimate and personal level longs for peace.

The church to which Paul wrote may not have been the church at Ephesus. Biblical scholars are unsure exactly to which church Paul was writing. It may have been that it was a circular letter simply sent to all the churches for the edification of whomever might read it. But the destination is really unimportant.

The purpose is primary. Paul knew that within the church there was the absence of real, genuine, abiding, authentic peace. There was, as you know, a division in the church—a division which ran along the lines of Jews and Gentiles. The Jews were the upper crust; the Gentiles were the intruders. The Jews were the circumcised; the Gentiles were the uncircumcised. The Jews had been there a long time; the Gentiles had just gained entrance. The Jews understood the impact and the importance of the ceremonial law; the Gentiles were babes, just learning this new religion. As a result, there was something in that community which created a sense of strife and, to be sure, created or caused the absence of peace.

You do remember that the temple at Jerusalem was a temple divided. It was not simply divided spiritually, but it was indeed divided physically. The temple had all kinds of classes of people. The Jews could only go so far, and then there was a wall. And beyond that wall sat the women. And beyond that wall sat the Gentiles. Every man behind a wall.

The wall. The wall. The wall created division. The wall created strife. The wall meant separation. The wall divided husbands from wives. The wall divided men from women. The wall divided Jews from Gentiles, and therefore there was no peace.

Walls. Walls are important. They are a part of the biblical legacy. You recall that it was Isaiah who declared that a watchman ought to stand on the wall to warn the city of the danger that lurked on the outside, to warn them of the advancing enemy. The watchman's job was also to stand on the wall to tell those on the inside of the city of the danger that was within.

The wall. Important in the history of Israel. You do recall that Nehemiah, in the midst of the Exile, received a word that somehow the walls of the old city, of the old temple, had fallen down, that the gates had been destroyed by fire. It was then that Nehemiah requested of the king permission to go home to rebuild the walls and restore the gates to their former position, as he put it, "in order that we be no more a reproach to our people." You remember from the Book of Ezra that Zerubbabel had the assignment of rebuilding the wall. And while others counseled with him about the advisability of coming down from the wall, he declared, "I cannot come down from the wall because he has assigned me to this task and to this charge."

Walls. Walls are funny things.

Walls not only invade our lives physically, but also affect our lives emotionally. They influence our lives mentally. Walls bother our lives psychologically. Are you aware of the wall in your life? Are you aware of the wall that lurks in your own mind?

Let me remind you that a wall is, in the first instance, *a defense mechanism*. The wall is designed to shut out. It protects me from you. A wall defends me from being known for what I am. If there is no wall, you can see my weakness and I can see your weakness, and therefore, to defend myself, to protect myself, to shield myself, I build a wall.

A wall. A wall also *prevents communication*. A wall prevents communication because, you see, as long as a wall exists I can possibly know that you are talking, but I cannot understand what you are saying. And, as long as I don't understand what you are saying, then there is no communication, and where there is no communication, there can be no peace.

A wall. A wall is not only a defense mechanism and not only does a wall prevent communication, but a wall also *prevents sight*. I, unfortunately, do not have x-ray vision. If I could, I would go into a telephone booth, change my robe to a Superman outfit, and take on my eyes of x-ray vision in order to look through your wall. But somehow the wall is there as a barrier to keep me from seeing you and also to keep you from seeing me. When I cannot see you, I cannot sense you. I cannot understand you. I cannot appreciate you.

> As long as the wall is there, I cannot see the smile on your face and therefore share in your joy.

> As long as the wall is there, I cannot see the frown on your face and therefore participate in your pain.

> As long as the wall is there, I cannot see the tear that flows down your cheek, and therefore I am insulated from your hurt.

> As long as the wall is there, I have a defense mechanism. I cannot see you, I cannot hear you, there is no communication, and therefore, because our relationship is incomplete, because our relationship is not full, because I have not really sought to share with you and you have not sought to legitimately share with me—therefore, there is no peace.

And so, these walls are destructive to the very purpose and priorities of the church. Remember that the wall divided the circumcised from the uncircumcised, men from women, Jews from Gentiles—separated people in the palace of God. What does it say? It says to us that there is a danger in *compartmentalized Christianity.* Walls create compartments. Walls create the rooms of our own personal religiosity. The problem comes whenever one segment interferes with the other. The problem comes when those who are supposed to be in one compartment move over and intervene and intersect into the compartment of the other. Therefore, we have separate choirs because we cannot all sing together. We have separate clubs and organizations, and cliques, and personal arrangements, and friends, because we are comfortable in our own compartmentalized Christianity.

He did not say, "Upon this rock I will build organizations."

He did not say, "Upon this rock I will build clubs."

He said, "Upon this rock I will build my church."

But as long as we are comfortable with our compartments, there is no peace!

*   *   *

My friends, consider the wall. There are two kinds of walls. There is, first of all, a bearing wall. A bearing wall is a wall you cannot do without. A bearing wall is designed to bear the weight of the structure. The wall with the window in it is a bearing wall because it holds up the weight of the roof. But it cannot be a bearing wall unless it is inextricably, fundamentally connected to the foundation. Now, if the wall that is around your life is not connected to the foundation, it is not a bearing wall. If the walls around your life are not connected to the rock, it will not sustain the weight of your problems, your difficulties, your trials; it will not sustain the weight of your tribulations. You need to be connected to the rock. "For other foundation can no man lay than that which is laid, which is Jesus Christ" (1 Corinthians 3:11). There is a bearing wall.

There is also this other wall of which Ephesians speaks. It is the middle wall. It is the interior wall. You can move that wall, and the building will still stand. Now, the problem with the interior wall is that we create them. We make up our own interior walls. We make up our own middle walls. And what is the middle wall? The middle wall is there because discrimination is there. The middle wall is there because hatred is there . . . envy is there . . . strife is there. And as long as there is a middle wall, there is no peace!

Throughout the Scriptures God is about the business of doing something about the wall. When the children of Israel made it to the Promised Land, the first thing that God had to do was to deal with the wall.

> Joshua! Joshua! There's a wall, Joshua. Joshua, there are some folk on the inside. Some on the outside. Joshua, there is a wall. The haves are divided from the have-nots. Joshua, there is a wall. The upper crust are divided from the no-crust. Joshua, there is a wall. The popular are divided from the unpopular. Joshua, get your regiments and get seven trumpets and walk around the wall for seven days and blow your trumpet seven times because the wall, the wall must come down.

As long as there is a wall, there is no peace! God is always dealing with the wall.

> "Daniel! Who is the king, Daniel?"
> "Belshazzar is the king."
> "What's he doing, Daniel?"
> "He's having a party. They're sipping wine and eating cheese."
> "What's going on, Daniel?"
> "They're making merry."
> "Daniel, where are they?"
> "They're in the palace."
> "Daniel, is there a wall? Daniel, is there a wall in the palace?"
> "Yes, Lord, there is a wall."
> "Well, Daniel, I'm not going down there. I don't have time to put up with the foolishness. I wouldn't send my whole body down to Belshazzar's party, but I will send my finger. I'll send my finger to the party, just so it can write, MENE, MENE, TEKEL, UPHARSIN."

Your kingdom has been divided. You have been weighed in the balance and found wanting. All because there is a wall. There is a wall in the kingdom, and as long as the wall is there, there is no peace!

The apostle Paul says that Jesus saw the wall that divided men from women, the circumcised from the uncircumcised, Jews from Gentiles. He says that He broke down the middle wall of partition.

How are you going to have your walls broken down? The wall is only broken down once you acknowledge your humanity, once you realize that you are no more than anyone else. Your wall comes down when you acknowledge that there is nothing to hide and no defense mechanism to secure you. "All we like sheep have gone astray; we have turned every one to his own way." The wall comes down when you quickly acknowledge that because of your sin, you too are in need of forgiveness. Once you realize your own need for forgiveness, your walls, your obstructions, your barriers have to come down.

*   *   *

This sermon is complete except for the fact that if I left it at this point, it would be a word of judgment only. And where there is God's judgment, there is also God's justice. Wherever God sits in judgment, He also holds out a plan of redemption. If there were no plan of redemption, then we would all be left for the rest of our days to live in our compartmentalized version of Christianity.

We need a word just now that will be redemptive for this hour. And the word is that God never leaves us with the middle walls in our lives, because of something that we put into every middle wall. Every middle wall that you've ever seen in your life has one thing in it: it has a door! If there were no door in a middle wall, we would be caught in a rat maze, we would be left to go round and round but never find a way out. There must be a door. There *is* a door. It is connected to your heart. But nobody will come bursting in. Nobody will break down your door. The lock is not on the outside. The lock is on the inside. And Jesus says: "Behold, I stand at the door and knock." I'm knocking on your middle wall. And if you will open up, I will come in and sup with you and you with Me.

Is there peace in the presence of these middle walls? Read again what Paul says to the Ephesians: *"For he is our peace."* Apart from Him there is no peace. Apart from the presence of Christ in your life, there is no peace. Apart from the power of God in my life, there is no peace. But when love comes in, when grace comes in, when power comes in, when sanctification comes in, when justification comes in, when the Holy Ghost comes in, I have peace . . . peace . . . peace . . . I have peace which passes all understanding.

David, what did you say?

> I was glad when they said unto me, Let us go into the house of the LORD. Our feet shall stand within thy gates, O Jerusalem. Jerusalem is builded as a city that is compact together: Whither the tribes go up, the tribes of the LORD, unto the testimony of Israel, to give thanks unto the name of the LORD. For there are set thrones of judgment, the thrones of the house of David. Pray for the peace of Jerusalem: they shall prosper that love thee. Peace be within thy walls and prosperity within thy palaces (Psalm 122:1–7).

He is, He is, He is our peace!

> I'm tired and I'm weary, but I must toil on
> Till the Lord comes and calls me away.
> Where the morning is bright and the Lamb is the light
> And the night is as fair as the day.
>
> There will be peace in the valley for me someday.
> There will be peace in the valley for me.
> I pray no sorrow, no sadness, nor trouble will be;
> There will be peace in the valley for me!
>
> *Thomas Dorsey*

EPILOGUE

Of the many sermons which I preached during the storm, "In Pursuit of Peace" was probably the most meaningful for me. I am a manuscript preacher, and I spend many hours constructing each sermon. This sermon, however, was delivered extemporaneously. I had come to the pulpit with only the barest of an outline, but with a burning burden in my soul for a sense of peace which had eluded me and the congregation as well. The sermon as it is presented here is a tape transcription of a word which came "in due season" for both pastor and people. (Bear in mind, of course, that no matter how faithful one is to the actual sermon text, there is something of the spirit that is lost in the translation when it moves from the oral to the written word. Sermons are instruments to be heard and experienced within the context of corporate worship.)

The primary lesson learned from this experience was that preaching through a storm requires an accentuation of the positive at every level. Preachments when they appear negative (even unintentionally) can only produce negative effects. As a result, the hearer and the listener run the risk of leaving more depressed than they were when they entered. To preach a positive word, often in spite of the storm, is the essence of the phrase "the Good News."

Sound preaching is never achieved in isolation. It must be understood and evaluated in the context of living worship. This means that the preacher must also be concerned about the setting in which preaching takes place. On more than one occasion I came to the preaching moment, standing with Bible in hand, and found the atmosphere so thick and tense, so negative in its impact, that something was required to alter the situation for the good of the whole. Many members of the congregation did not understand my motive when I became aggressively involved in the preliminary worship service.

Often I would ask members during the singing of a particularly moving congregational hymn to turn and shake hands with one another. I would then leave the pulpit and walk the aisles, shaking hands with friend and foe alike. The purpose and intent was, of course, to make a bold statement that no matter what our personal or individual differences, we had come to the house of God for the purpose of praising Him. Worship is a moment when all other matters must be pushed aside in the expectant hope that God Himself, through His Holy Spirit, will infuse the congregation with the "burning bush" of His presence and thereby purify His people of any residue of recrimination and mistrust and bring His perfect peace.

The effect of this new model of worship ministry was significant. It affected the worshiping spirit of the congregation and, for many, brought about a new sense of warmth and relaxation that are still operative in our worship today. All of this is a part of maintaining wholesome relationships within the household of faith. It is an effective means of living with and preaching through the stormy cataclysms of church confusion and doubt.

> We share each other's joys,
> Our mutual burdens bear;
> And often for each other flows
> A sympathizing tear.
>
> *John Fawcett*

THE EYE OF THE STORM

PROLOGUE

It was a time for rejoicing in my season of storm even though I did not know it and could not sense it. I had nearly come to midpoint in the storm that had tossed me fore and aft, from stem to stern. It appeared that the storm was finally about to subside. The Historic Landmarks Commission had released the church from the threat of imposed restrictions, and even through the storm, to the surprise of most, the church had amassed an additional five hundred thousand dollars, bringing our assets up to the church-imposed requirement of one million dollars before construction could begin. It was now our joy to say at last, "All things are ready!"

Not quite. There is often a momentary lull in a storm while the currents shift and the winds regather themselves to strike with even greater rage and intensity. So it was with us. The calm was followed by an even fiercer onslaught. Accusatory letters were mailed to the congregation charging, among other things, fiscal irresponsibility and questioning the integrity of the entire process. It was distressing to see new names appear as signatories, names of people who had previously seemed supportive. I began to wonder if the support base was now eroding before my very eyes.

A date had been set for the last service of worship to be held in the soon-to-be demolished sanctuary, and the choice before us was clear: either stand still and wait for the storm to subside, or move forward in the power of the Lord and in the strength of His might. The choice was not easily made.

This cancerous conflict was exacerbated by yet another unexpected element of the storm for which I was not emotionally or spiritually prepared. One day at my office I received a phone call. A voice I did not recognize said, "Do not go to the pulpit again. If you tear the church down, you will be dead." Then the phone went dead.

What are we doing here? I thought. *Is this the way people act who claim to be Christians? Have we really come to this?* The questions begged for answers I was unable to give.

It was not a happy moment in my ministry when I sat in my office, the walls seeming to close in on me as I shared with my board chairpersons the dilemma in which I now found myself. The glass top on my desk was cold to the touch of my forehead, and I found my face wet with tears . . . tears of anger, confusion, anxiety, and doubt. Somewhere . . . I remembered the Scripture . . . I had read the counsel, "Touch not mine anointed, and do my prophets no harm."

I hoped I was not the only one who had read that passage of Scripture, and I wondered if perhaps I needed to reexamine its meaning. Is this what Jesus meant when He wept over Jerusalem, "O Jerusalem, Jerusalem, thou that killest the prophets, and stonest them which are sent unto thee" (Matthew 23:37)? Faced with a genuine threat, I discovered I was not prepared to die.

With characteristic compassion, the board chairpersons decided that I should not be present for worship on the following Sunday morning. It was Women's Day, and a guest speaker was scheduled, so my absence could easily be tolerated.

I left the city hurriedly—only my wife knew my exact location—and checked into a hotel under an assumed name. My hotel room was a bright, warm, well-appointed, spacious "hideout," but I was ill at ease. I knew I was not safe. I had only taken up residence in the eye of the storm.

The eye of the storm is a strange phenomenon of nature. While the storm rages without, at the center, at the core of the storm, there is an area of perfect peace and tranquility. It is so still in the eye of the storm that one is hard pressed to believe that the storm actually exists. Living in the eye of the storm can be comforting . . . but only for a moment. There are certain hazards in the eye of the storm, and any preacher living in or heading into his own personal storm should know about them.

The first hazard of the eye of the storm is that *it deceives one into believing that the storm does not exist.* It is a "never-never land" where all is sweetness and light. I assure you, however, that the storm is still there. To believe, if only for a moment, that the storm is no longer present is to play ecclesiastical ostrich with your head steadfastly buried in the sand of your own destruction. It's like believing that if you pull the covers over your head, the sun will not rise to interrupt your rest. The preacher is on a treadmill of unending tragedy as long as he refuses to admit the existence of the storm.

The second hazard of the eye of the storm is that *it isolates the preacher* from those people or resources which could aid in his rescue. In a storm one needs to remain in the company of friends who can provide essential support. An isolated pastor, one cut off from the support of others, can only chafe at the internal festering sores of self-depreciation and low self-esteem. An isolated pastor is vulnerable to the storm's fierce onslaught.

Preacher-pastors are often among the loneliest people in the world. They appear to have an inborn insecurity. It is difficult to know whom to trust, whom to believe, with whom to share innermost thoughts. To live in the eye of the storm is to live in a self-imposed exile, a "Patmos" of choice, which is not wholesome either psychologically or spiritually.

The third and most serious hazard of living in the eye of the storm is that *it places the preacher in the category of the fearful prophet.* Much in the manner of the prophet Elijah, a subject to which we shall later return, the preacher is perceived by others and even perceived by himself as one afraid to face the enemy, intimidated by a mortal adversary, unable to live by the word of faith which he preaches. To live fearfully in the eye of a storm is to make the lie of everything the preacher stands for and is an insult to the promise of divine protection and intervention. If the Lord is truly my light and my salvation, "whom shall I fear?" If the Lord is truly the strength of my life, "of whom shall I be afraid?" One's fear for self is made manifest by the presence of similar fear in others.

With a strong sense of obligation, but also with real fear, I returned to the pulpit for the last sermon in the old church (and others to follow) in a bulletproof vest and escorted by an armed bodyguard. We had, indeed, come to this. The eye of the storm was not a source of salvation. I came to the pulpit of this noble and God-blessed church with what I hoped would be a word of courage and confidence—even in the midst of the storm.

Sermon: CONCERNING THIS HOUSE

Concerning this house which thou art in building, if thou wilt walk in my statutes, and execute my judgments, and keep all my commandments to walk in them; then will I perform my word with thee, which I spake unto David thy father: And I will dwell among the children of Israel, and will not forsake my people Israel. So Solomon built the house, and finished it (1 Kings 6:12–14).

I stand, for a final time, in this sacred place of preaching, cradled, as it were, between these consecrated walls which have been a witness to worship for nearly a century of time. I am aware of the legacy which sustains us, the present which surrounds us, and the future which beckons us. God be praised that the foresight of our parents yet lives in the vision of their children. God be praised for this field planted by preachers of years gone by. One planted, still others watered, and tonight God still yields the increase. God be praised for the hills and the valleys of our years. They alone have given meaning to our singing:

> Through many dangers, toils and snares
> I have already come;
> 'Tis grace hath brought me safe thus far,
> And grace will lead me home.
> *John Newton*

God be praised for the majesty of the moment in which we are met.

Permit me then to call upon your patience, as I wanted to share a word with you "concerning this house." More particularly, I wanted to have a word with King Solomon. I wanted to share a moment of conversation with a king who is experienced in this business of building a temple for the Lord. If you don't mind tonight, I thought it might be helpful to exchange ideas and insights with someone who knows what it is to mount the challenge of creative construction. I really thought it might be to our advantage to review this matter of kingdom-building with a king who has already lifted up from the ground an edifice for the King of Kings. I wanted to have a word with King Solomon.

Solomon, you will recall, reigned over the kingdom of Israel from 931 to 910 B.C. Solomon was the second son of David and Bathsheba. He knew what it was to sit on a pinnacle of renown, reared as a royal prince who came to power in the tenderness of his youth. Nathan the prophet saw in Solomon the symbol of eternal forgiveness, and so gave him one additional name, Jedidiah, for he was the beloved of God. You will recall, additionally, that Solomon was known for his wisdom. It is said that Solomon was the composer of three thousand proverbs as well as a thousand songs. Solomon was skilled in matters of governmental and military administration, and in the arena of international diplomacy and trade, Solomon knew no peer.

But that's not why I wanted to have dialogue with Solomon. I wanted to look to Solomon tonight because I thought that we might do well, and I might do well, to have an understanding of Solomon's wisdom. Solomon made his way to Gibeon, and there in a dream God asked Solomon what he would like to be given. Said Solomon, "I want an understanding mind. . . . Give therefore thy servant an understanding heart to judge thy people that I may discern between good and evil." And so, perhaps I ought to say at the outset that you cannot build the house of God unless you have an understanding heart, and I declare that with it you will become acquainted with good and evil.

What a tragedy it was that Solomon had to build the temple in the first place! By all rights, David should have built it. David wanted to build it. God gave him time to build it, for David reigned over Israel for forty years. But somehow David's building plans never got off the drawing board. Solomon could easily have passed on the building plans to someone else. And that's why I wanted to talk with him, because I know he didn't have an easy time of it.

I know Solomon had a hard time, because he had to deal with the same folk that Moses tried to lead into the Promised Land. These were the church members that Moses had standing at the Red Sea with freedom in their grasp and liberty in their eyesight. These were the same folk that told Moses, "We should have died back in Egypt. We were doing all right with our flesh pots back in Pharaoh's brickyard. At least back in Egypt we had bread, and here we are out here, and we're hungry. Back in Egypt we had a balanced budget because we had no budget; we had full employment because everyone was a slave. And here you've brought us out here with death behind us and hard times ahead of us. Let's go back to Egypt."

I feel sorry for Solomon. I'm glad I don't have to face these kinds of problems. For those with whom he dealt were the direct descendants of the tribes of Israel that finally made it to the Promised Land. Even then, however, when Moses had them looking over into a land that flowed with milk and honey, Caleb and Joshua were the co-chairmen of the committee that went to spy out the land. He had them at the gateway of God's promise and some folk said, "We're not going." My Bible tells me that the tribe of Reuben, the tribe of Gad, and one-half of the tribe of Manasseh never made it. They preferred the security of what used to be rather than the glory of what would be. These were the same folk with whom Solomon had to build the temple, and that's why I wanted to share just a word with Solomon the king.

It just concerns me, it interests me, it intrigues me as to why Solomon would build in the first place. He did not have the resources to build. He had to send thirty thousand men to import stones from the quarries of Phoenicia. He had to import wood from the pines and cedars of Lebanon. He ran out of money and had to take out a second mortgage, and at the same time he was trying to trade off wheat and oil in order to get lumber and gold from Hiram. He needed eight thousand men to build the temple and seven years to complete it.

I don't know why he took the risk to build when any economist could have told him that he did not have the resources to build. That's why I needed to talk with Solomon to find out what he had in his mind that made him want to build when everything and everybody around him said, "Don't do it."

*   *   *

No doubt Solomon built because he was concerned about the church. Without a church, no one would know what Israel thought about the God whom they served. Without a temple, they would not honor the faith of their fathers Abraham, Isaac, and Jacob. Without a sanctuary, there would be no gathering place where the saints of God could praise and pray. Solomon was concerned about the church.

That leads me to say that we ought to be concerned about the church. I am concerned that unless the church is moving to new vistas of ministry, the creature will lose touch with the Creator. I am concerned that if our persuasion is only to live in the past, we shall be no more than curators of ecclesiastical antique shops. I am concerned about the church. The church must always be responsive to the age in which it lives. Truman W. Potter has suggested that the most serious indictment of the contemporary church may be that we are living as citizens of the space age and at the same time trying to run the church as a horse-and-buggy operation. Like Solomon, I am concerned about the church.

Without the church, where is the place of encounter between man and his Maker?

Without the church, where is the soul's shaping ground?

Without the church, what shall our children know as their father's praying ground?

Without the church, where shall we touch the garment of the living God?

Because of the church I can say tonight, "A day in thy courts is better than a thousand elsewhere. I would rather be a doorkeeper in the house of my God, than dwell in the tents of wickedness."

And so I wanted to talk with Solomon tonight because he may have some instructive insights on this matter of building a house for the Lord.

Now the Bible says, "And the word of the Lord came to Solomon . . ." that leads me to say that before you begin to build, you'd better be certain that you have a word from the Lord.

Don't come out here by yourself. It's going to get lonely sometime.

Don't step out on your own strength. You'll get weak sometime.

Don't get hung up on your ego. You'll be hated sometime.

Don't move off because of your money. You'll be broke sometime.

If you go, you'd better go because God said, "Go."

If we build, we ought to build because it's His will and not our will.

The mountains are high. The valleys are deep. The rivers are wide. The bridges are broken. Friends are few. Enemies are many. Interest is high. Money is hard to come by. I hear Solomon saying, "You'd better be sure you heard a word from the Lord." My father David told me:

Except the Lord build the house they labour in vain that build it: except the Lord keep the city the watchman waketh but in vain (Psalm 127:1).

This Book says, "The word of the LORD came to Solomon, saying, Concerning this house which thou art in building. . . ." In other words, do you have any thoughts concerning the nature of this house? I know you have your architectural design and I know you have your engineering specifications and I know you have made your plans and your projections, but you ought to know something concerning this house you're about to build.

And so, I hope you'll forgive me tonight, but I have certain revelation of the Holy Spirit that I wanted to share with you concerning this house.

*   *   *

The first thing I need to tell you is that we all know that everybody will not help in the building of the house. And the reason for that is not because they're stubborn, and not because they're evil, not because they're recalcitrant and vindictive. The reason is that a whole lot of folk have "bandwagon religion." They want to wait and see what happens before they commit themselves. They want to keep their options open. They always want to stay away from the possibility of failure just so they can say, "I told you so." But when victory comes around, they'll be the first to say, "I was with you all the time."

The second thing I need to tell you concerning this house is that it is a house!

The church is a house, designed as the dwelling place of God.

The church is a house, the residence of the people of God.

The church is a house, a frequent landing pad for the satellite of the Holy Spirit.

The church is a house. It is not a country club for the rich. It is a house for those who hunger and thirst after righteousness.

The church is a house. It is not a sanctuary for pseudo-intellectuals and the ne'er-do-well intelligentsia. It is a house where all men and women are equal at the feet of God.

The church is a house. It is not an exclusive club, but an inclusive fellowship.

The church is a house. It is not a place for sanctimonious sewing circles and socially acceptable tea sipping.

The church is a hospital for the sick, a saving center for sinners, and a lighthouse for the lost. The church is a house.

And when a new meeting place is built, it must be as an aid to worship and not the object of worship. The bricks and mortar are an aid to worship, not the object of worship. The choir is an aid to worship, not the object of worship. The preacher is a leader of worship and not the object of worship. The Bible is a guide to worship, but it is not the object of worship.

God alone is to be worshiped here. Not the place, not the structure, not the stones, not the name, not the history, not the heritage, not the land. God alone is worthy to be praised. The church is a house. It is God's house.

*   *   *

Look at what this Word says. I wanted to talk with Solomon tonight, for maybe he could tell us how God's house can be built. Solomon suggests that if you want to build the house, God says there are three things you must do.

The first thing you must do is to walk in His statutes. Now, to walk in the statutes means you must be willing to be governed by God's law. You must be willing to be disciplined by God's law. You cannot build God's house where there is no discipline. The apostle Paul told the church at Corinth that all things must be done decently and in order. God has some laws. God has some standards of conduct. God has some dictates of discipline. God has some ordinances of order. You want to know what God's statute is? Ask Brother Micah. "He hath shewed thee, O man, what is good; and what doth the LORD require of thee, but to do justly, and to love mercy, and to walk humbly with thy God?" (Micah 6:8).

Not only must you walk in his statutes, but God told Solomon, you have to "execute my judgments." We don't like the word of judgment, but I'm persuaded by the Holy Ghost that God has a word of judgment for the church.

Just because you look pious, there is a word of judgment.

Never mind how right and righteous you've convinced your little nest of friends you are, there is a word of judgment.

It makes no difference how important you look in your uniform or how resplendent you look in your robe, there is a word of judgment.

Jesus went down to this same temple that Solomon was building and found money changers robbing the poor and stealing from the blind. Jesus told them, "You forgot this is a house. And it's my Father's house. It is my house. And my house shall be called a house of prayer, but you have made it a den of thieves." If we're going to stay away from the judgment of God, there had better be some prayer in his house. The church ought to be a seven-day prayer meeting. Every organization in the church ought to be a prayer meeting.

Tithing clubs ought not tithe till they have prayer meeting.

Ushers ought not come to the floor till they have prayer meeting.

Choirs ought not put on their robes till they have prayer meeting.

Deacons ought not to be deacons till they learn the worth of prayer in prayer meeting.

The Holy Ghost won't come till we have prayer meeting. You can't build God's house without prayer.

Joseph Scriven said:

O what peace we often forfeit,
O what needless pain we bear,
All because we do not carry
Everything to God in prayer!

Unless the church is a praying church, we stand under the judgment of God.

And so I hear God telling Solomon, "If you want to build this house, walk in my statutes, execute my judgments, and then follow my commandments." God still has a commandment for the church. And His commandment is to be found in the sure Word of God. The rich young ruler came to Jesus and asked, "Good Master, what must I do to gain eternal life?" Jesus said, "Follow the commandments." A lawyer came to

Jesus and said, "We know you're talking about the commandments of Moses, but just which is the greatest commandment?" He heard Jesus say, "Thou shalt love the Lord thy God with all thy heart, and with all thy soul, and with all thy mind. . . . And the second is like unto it, Thou shalt love thy neighbour as thyself" (Matthew 22:37, 39).

You still want to know what the commandment is? Jesus told His disciples one day, "A new commandment I give unto you, That you love one another; as I have loved you. . . . By this shall all men know that ye are my disciples, if ye have love one to another" (John 13:34–35).

You cannot build a church where there is no love.

> Though I speak with the tongues of men and of angels, and have not charity, I am become as sounding brass, or a tinkling cymbal (1 Corinthians 13:1).

So Solomon built the house and finished it.
He didn't just start it, he finished it.
He didn't just break ground for it, he finished it.
He didn't just talk about it, he finished it.
I tell you, church, let's finish it. Like Nehemiah on the wall. Don't come down, let's finish it!

EPILOGUE

To analyze this sermon briefly it is fair and accurate to say that it was strident in tone and in many ways a frontal attack on the listeners. Clearly, the anger boiling within me found a way out through this sermon. I wondered, on deeper reflection, if as preacher I was fighting others or myself. The tone of the whole sermon in many ways accounts for some unwarranted thematic shifts as well as some rather poor exegesis, particularly on the word "judgments." Perhaps the note here ought to be that, while preaching through a storm, and precisely because of the storm, the preacher must never become homiletically careless or fail to do his homework. Storm or no storm, there is no substitute for sound preaching.

I remember hearing my father say on more than one

occasion that the preacher has not really been effective until he makes someone mad. If that be the case, then "Concerning This House" achieved its goal. Those who were opposed to the building effort were discomfited, and those who had been supportive of the process were enthusiastic in their response. It is certain that the sermon served to clarify my position as pastor and was a strong statement of my personal beliefs, whether anyone joined me in them or not. It was certain that from that point on I would no longer live in the eye of the storm. The lines were drawn. The gauntlet had been thrown down. I was to experience within the next two weeks a depth of disarray and confusion which I had not seen before nor ever wish to see again.

On a Tuesday evening, late in the month of November, a meeting of the congregation was held which would, to borrow a phrase from Franklin Roosevelt, "go down in infamy." The charges, the countercharges, questions, and controversy had incensed the congregation to a point where it appeared surely the church would split with no prospect for reconciliation.

This was the moment when I was most ready to give up. I was within a hairsbreadth of calling it quits. It seemed as if God must have had something else for me to do, some other purpose to fulfill. I was so anxious to bring this confusion to an end and save the church that I suggested to the congregation, as I had previously to the board, that we abandon the building project, return to the now-deserted and dismantled sanctuary, and try to begin again with a new understanding and a different set of terms and conditions.

Surprise! The vote to abandon the building program *failed!* Every attempt to return to the old sanctuary met with defeat. There was yet within the heretofore silent core of the congregation a significant majority of people committed to the achievement of this goal. I discovered—wonder of wonders— that the fight was not my own. I had been in the storm so long—but not alone. There were others who felt the need, shared the dream, and were determined not to let the church die such an ignominious death. Praise God! He is able! He still "gives power to the faint, and to them that have no might, He increases strength" precisely in the midst of the storm!

PREACHING THROUGH A STORM

As I look back upon it now, I am amazed by how seriously I took myself and my storm. Charles Adams of the Hartford Memorial Church in Detroit suggested, while preaching to our congregation, that often what we perceive to be a major storm is really no more than a little wind, albeit a contrary wind.

How seriously we take ourselves! Have we forgotten "Give no thought for tomorrow"? Have we forgotten "Be careful for nothing; but in every thing by prayer and supplication with thanksgiving let your requests be made known unto God. And the peace of God, which passeth all understanding, shall keep your hearts and minds through Christ Jesus" (Philippians 4:6–7)? It really *is* His church. He builds it and protects it either with us or without us, and no matter what the storm, His will is always achieved.

In a recent conference on ministerial leadership sponsored by the National Congress of Black Churches, one participant observed that the Lord always delivers the church to the pastor in a storm. Many a person has been called to serve a church, but often only after a time of storm-tossed tension does the minister become pastor. In a sense, then, God seems to use the creative tension of storms as a means of solidifying the pastor in his office in the mind and heart of both pastor and people. While we may not understand it, the storms of the ministry serve to make us what we are and are the molder of what we shall become.

> We are tossed and driven on the restless sea of time;
> Somber skies and howling tempests oft succeed a bright
>   sunshine;
> But we're trusting in the Lord, and according to His Word,
> We will understand it better by and by!
>
> *Charles A. Tindley*

THE IDENTITY OF EVIL

PROLOGUE

In his daily work, a pastor deals with a variety of human personalities. The timid and the aggressive, the independent and the dependent, the gregarious spirit and the recluse, the intelligent and those of average and below-average intelligence, the substance abuser and the alcoholic, "straights" and "gays," males and females—they are all part of the human walk, and the pastor's call is to minister to them all.

Unlike the lawyer or the doctor, the pastor is not able to specialize in a particular congregation characterized by a particular mindset. To do so would be antithetical to the demands of the all-inclusive gospel and would, I suspect, be a most boring theological and ecclesiastical enterprise.

Moreover, a pastor discovers soon enough that congregations, like individuals, also have their own personalities. The personality of a specific congregation may be warm or cold, reserved or emotive, socially active or self-contained, given to intense Bible study or perhaps marked by an emphasis on music ministries. It can be a fighting church or a loving church. The same personality traits found in individuals may similarly be found in whole congregations. At times the mixture of personalities within a church may produce a spirit that is wholesome and sweet. Conversely the mixture of unwholesome personalities within a congregation may be volatile and may bear within the corpus the seed of its own destruction and death.

It is essential that a pastor come to understand the forces at work in the human personality and in the congregation. By this knowledge, gained over a span of years, he is able to minister effectively and meaningfully in the spirit of our Christ.

It is particularly important that he understand evil. Every pastor engaged in ministry will encounter evil—whether in individuals or in the character of the congregation. He must be prepared to identify it and to deal with it.

In the face of evil opposition, a pastor may cynically (though understandably) conclude that man is innately evil, that there is a "bad seed" at the core of all men. Certainly such a view is common in theological and philosophical history. If, on the other hand, we take another theological view that in each of us, no matter how misguided or depraved, there is a spark of divinity in our humanity,* if we side with the maxim that "there is some bad in the best of us and some good in the worst of us," then we may be led to the conclusion that none of us (neither pastor nor people) is beyond reclamation and redemption through the saving grace of Jesus Christ. If we honestly believe, as I think we must, that the Christ whom we preach is able to love the unlovable, wash the dirty, and redeem those of low estate, in like manner we must not give up on what Reinhold Niebuhr has called "the nature and destiny of man."

Over the past few years I have come to an affirmation of my own belief that there is an evil influence in the world. Christian theology informs my position, for the Bible is insistent upon the presence and power of what it describes as the ultimate manifestation of evil and has named this force Satan or the Devil. Noted author and psychiatrist M. Scott Peck

---

*I am aware that the divinity-in-humanity argument is on tenuous theological ground. God created us as humans; He did not make us divine. The Barthian position states that there is a qualitative difference or distinction between God and man. Nevertheless, for me, the point made above remains meaningful and, as it was my initial impression, I have chosen to permit the observation to stand.

has written a book entitled *People of the Lie: The Hope for Healing Human Evil*. In his book, Peck acknowledges and seeks to authenticate the presence and reality of evil and defines it most clearly as either an internal or external force which is antithetical to life itself.

This chapter seeks to aid the preacher-pastor in understanding and identifying this evil force. The effort is fraught with danger. I could easily be accused of branding certain persons in my congregation as the personification of evil. That is not my intent. I am not qualified clinically nor would I presume to make such judgments. Indeed, this entire book may appear to be an exercise in finger-pointing or fault-fixing. That is not my purpose. In fact, I would join with Norman Cousins citing Dostoevsky in acknowledging that "nothing is easier than to denounce the evil-doer; nothing is more difficult than to understand him."[1]

Still, we must be able to identify evil so we can understand it. We must do it in the hope that we may, through the preaching event, seek the redemption of evil-doers. Failing that, we must do it so that we ourselves do not become immobilized by the presence and power of evil in others.

I cannot possibly give you a complete analysis of evil in this brief chapter, but I wish to share three insights I gained from my own encounter with evil in my congregation.

First of all, the preacher-pastor should understand at the very beginning that "what you see" may not be "what you get." Superficial and surface judgments of persons within the congregation may lead you to believe that you are dealing with a lamb, when in fact you are walking with a wolf. Did not Jesus warn us of "wolves in sheep's clothing"? Take the warning seriously! Evil does exist in the church—in my church, in your church, and in every church. The presence of evil can be seen, heard, felt, and experienced. The problem is that evil always poses as something it is not. Peck explains:

> Since the primary motive of the evil is disguise, one of the places evil people are most likely to be found is within the church. What better way to conceal one's evil from oneself, as

well as from others, than to be a deacon or some other highly visible form of Christian within our culture.[2]

Second, you will find in persons of evil nature a preoccupation with failure. What makes their insistence upon failure so demonic is that they do it under the guise of intense religiosity. My experience teaches that one is never confronted by an evil opponent who has not convinced him or herself—along with other allies—of the moral and spiritual purity of their intent. Once again Peck is on target when he suggests that

> the evil attack others instead of facing their own failures. . . . They are often busily engaged in hating and destroying . . . life—usually in the name of righteousness. . . . The evil are pathologically attached to the status quo of their own personalities, which in their narcissism they consciously regard as perfect.[3]

Finally, the evil, though responsible for their acts, are, in the spirit of Christ, deserving of empathetic understanding. Primarily the evil are to be understood in this fashion because they do not have the psychological tools or internal resources to deal with the presence of evil in their lives. No doubt you will find that Cousins is right when he says:

> The enemy is a man (or woman) who not only believes in his own helplessness, but actually worships it. His main article of faith is that there are mammoth forces at work which the individual cannot possibly comprehend, much less alter or direct. And so he expends vast energies in attempting to convince other people that there is nothing they can do. He is an enemy because of the proximity of helplessness to hopelessness.[4]

Fundamentally, evil (sin) must be faced head-on. It must not be permitted to exist without a word of challenge or creative confrontation. It is highly unlikely that the preacher-pastor will be able to engage the truly evil in a meaningful counseling relationship, and it is equally unlikely that he will be able to make a psychological or psychiatric referral to a professional trained to handle this disease of the spirit. It may be consoling to suggest as did Jesus that "this kind goeth not out but by prayer and fasting" (Matthew 17:21), but the problem must be recognized, labeled, and dealt with for what it is—evil. The challenge to the preacher-pastor, as he understands the phenomenon, is to find more creative approaches to the problem of evil, based on biblical example, which will enable him to preach directly to evil and thereby speak directly to the storm.

In my case, I chose to address it head-on in Joseph's words to his brothers.

Sermon: RECYCLED EVIL

But as for you, ye thought evil against me; but God meant it unto good, to bring to pass, as it is this day, to save much people alive (Genesis 50:20).

The epochal story of Joseph is stretched like a tapestry over the concluding pages of the book known to us as Genesis. Joseph, child of Jacob and Rachel, beloved in the eyes of his father, finds the narrative of his life and times told with vivid detail. So vivid, in fact, that the bold experiences of his life are as colorful as his coat of many colors. But the theme of Genesis is not Joseph—the theme of Genesis is God: what God is, what God requires, and ultimately how God acts in human history.

I think that our discussion today will be on solid ground if we begin with the understanding that the theme of Genesis is God.

From the creation of man on the banks of cosmic energy to the fall of man in Eden's garden, the theme of Genesis is God.

From the sin of Sodom and Gomorrah and the hesitation of Lot's wife to the arrogant tragedy of the Tower of Babel, the theme of Genesis is God.

From Abraham's urgent imperative to leave home without a road map to the advent of Isaac and the ensuing encounter on Mount Moriah, the theme of Genesis is God.

From the coming of Jacob and the birth of his twelve sons, who made up the twelve tribes of Israel, to the final dramatic encounter with Joseph, who gave food to his starving brothers in Egypt, the theme of Genesis is God: what God is, what God requires, and how God acts in human history. The theme, I say, the theme of Genesis is God.

And yet, while I understand the theme—and it is important that we understand the theme—I find here in this narrative of a lad named Joseph an undercurrent of implication which unnerves my psyche and unsettles my spirit. The story of Joseph disturbs me because it not only raises questions about man's relationship with man, but also causes a controversy down in the canyons of my conscience regarding God's purpose and intention for man and mankind. He who is of the opinion that the Joseph narrative is only there to tell of the misadventures of a young lad and his coat of many colors somehow has misunderstood the meaning of the text and has not carefully examined the word that is in the word behind the word. And that's why I wanted to share with you today this matter of implication and inference that is deeply imbedded and implanted in the Joseph story which raises questions and concerns in my mind about the nature and the destiny of man.

Perhaps you may not have previously identified this matter, but the Joseph story is designed to deal with the question of evil in the world. The question raised is, what do you do when the forces of evil are all about you? Perhaps you've had a question in your life. How does one respond when that which is iniquitous, and wicked, and sinful, and abominable, atrocious, enormous, and monstrous, shameful and scandalous, devilish, diabolical and damnable—what do you do when evil is all around you? I bring this matter to your attention primarily because the Joseph story raises the level of our consciousness to see clearly two alternating factors of human experience. The Joseph story looks at good and evil and holds them up in the light of contrast and contradiction.

I hope that you do not mind my bringing this matter to your attention, because there is no way to deny the reality of evil. There is no way to make evil less than evil—evil is evil. We are not very good at convincing ourselves that "evil is simply good in the making." It is not psychologically or intellectually satisfying to suggest that "sin is but the shadow of holiness." There is a reality to evil. To contrast good and evil it is not enough to say that one is substance and the other shadow; one is positive, the other negative; one is a fullness and the other emptiness.

On the contrary, wherever evil stands in the presence of goodness, there is a spiritual push and pull at work. There is, as it were, a cosmic conflict at work—bad will act negatively on one side and good will act positively on the other side, and what occurs is clash and conflict, tension and struggle, an eternal warfare between right and wrong, sin and holiness. The reality of evil is such that unless evil is understood and unless we have an adequate way to respond to the forces of evil, the very foundation of the moral government of God is being weighed in the balance and perhaps found wanting.

And so, perhaps there is an understanding of, or an acknowledgment of, some experience of evil in your life. It may well be that you have some questions you might like to raise regarding this matter of evil. You might want to ask, why does evil occur in the first place? It may be of considerable importance to your own spiritual health to ask how a loving God can permit evil in the world. And then, if God does permit evil when He could prevent evil, does He not then become evil?

I thought perhaps you might want to inquire, along with Jeremiah, why do the wicked prosper? Why is it that the forces of wrong, the doers of dirty deeds, the "fat cats" and the "slick mamas"—why is it that they seem to do better than anybody else? And then if I must adjust myself to the reality of evil, and if I have to live my life in the presence of evil, and if there is no way to escape the insulting assault of evil, what can one do with the reality of evil in one's life?

You perhaps had never seen or understood this question to be raised in the story of Joseph, so I wanted to see if we could briefly inquire about the Joseph story to see if we can find an answer to the questions we pose. I would not want you to forget for a moment that the theme of Genesis is God, but the story of Joseph is designed to instruct us in the matter of effectively dealing with the problem of evil.

I trust you have not forgotten the details of the life of Joseph. Joseph was hated by his brothers and despised because of his dreams. The presence of his coat of many colors caused his brothers to burn in hot jealousy against him. They stripped

Joseph of his coat and smeared goat's blood upon it and cast him into a pit to die. In a stroke of characteristic generosity, his brothers lifted him out of the pit and sold him to the Ishmaelites for the grand sum of twenty pieces of silver and doomed him to a life of slavery in Egypt.

You do remember this Joseph who wound up in the home of Potiphar, captain of the Egyptian guard. While there in the service of Potiphar, Potiphar's wife decided she had designs on Joseph. When she was unable to impugn his moral character and was unable, by her cunning and wily devices, to besmirch his reputation, Joseph wound up in prison, charged, tried, and convicted on trumped-up charges.

I really hope you have not forgotten Joseph. For it was this Joseph who, while in prison, made friends with the butler and the baker who were on death row with him. They discovered that Joseph had an uncanny ability to interpret dreams, and Joseph helped them through the use of his skill. The Book says that the chief baker was hanged, but the butler got out of prison on parole, but it also says the chief butler forgot Joseph.

I don't want you to forget Joseph, for here was a man who was hated by his brothers, sold into slavery, tricked by a woman, imprisoned on false charges, and forgotten in jail by the man he had befriended. Evil was all around him. Not misfortune. Not bad luck. Evil. His life is the record of multiplied evil. But somehow in the midst of the evil, God raised him up. In a pit, God raised him up. In slavery, God raised him up. Maligned and abused, God raised him up. In prison, God raised him up. He was without friends to count on, and yet God raised him up. He didn't do it, God did it. God raised him up to be the secretary of agriculture. In charge of the food in a time of famine, God raised him up. But I still want to know, what do you do when evil is all around you?

The Scripture requires that I tell you that after all this, evil was not finished in Joseph's life. For somehow, just at the time when it looked as if good had won the day, evil came back into his life. Evil came into Joseph's life in the form of death. The Book says that Jacob closed his eyes in death, having lived to see 110 years of mortal life, and they tell me they embalmed him and he was put in a coffin in Egypt. You must understand how important Jacob was. In Jacob had come much of the fulfillment of the promises of God.

Jacob's sons numbered twelve; they and their descendants would possess the Promised Land. Not only was Jacob important to his children, who would look back upon him as a patriarch to his people, but he was important to God. Jacob was so important to God that heaven set up a messenger service for him one night—and all night long, heaven had angels ascending and descending on a ladder that stretched from high heaven to low earth. Jacob was important. So important was Jacob that even God Himself wrestled with him all night long until the breaking of the day, and we hear Jacob say, "I'm not going to let You go until You bless me."

Jacob was important. So important was Jacob that God asked him, "What is your name?"

Said he, "My name is Jacob."

But God replied, "No longer shall your name be Jacob, your name shall be Israel because you have power with God, and with men you have prevailed."

Jacob was important to God, but now Jacob was dead. And I'm here to tell you that when death comes into your life, that's evil. When death steps up to your doorstep and snatches away that which you love more than life itself, death is life's ultimate evil. When whatever is important in your life dies, when death comes to your hopes and dreams, when death comes to that which makes getting up in the morning worthwhile, when death snatches away the joy in your life and the sunshine in your soul, you will understand that death is evil. And that's why I thought it might be helpful to examine this matter and see if we can determine the best direction to take when evil is in your life.

*　　*　　*

And so you do remember that Joseph now is in charge of the corn in Egypt. God has raised him up to be in charge of the grocery store just at the time when rations run out in Israel. His brothers have come back now and at last they have discovered his identity. Much to their amazement, they discovered that the man in charge of food stamps is the same man that they put in a pit one day and sold off into slavery. They discovered that the same man who had control over their future was the brother they had hated, the brother they had envied, the brother against whom they were jealous, the brother who had the same father as they. But now Jacob was dead. And I hear those brothers saying, "We're in trouble now. Jacob is dead, and he was the only thing that kept Joseph from us. Jacob is dead now, and Joseph can have his sweet revenge. Jacob is dead, and Joseph can have his payback now."

But those brothers came to Joseph saying, "We know that we've done wrong. And we know that we've sinned. We know that we've been the agents of that which is evil. And we just want you to know that we're your servants."

Candor makes me comment here that I do not know of a twentieth-century man or woman that would be willing to make the kind of confession these brothers made. It is, however, to their abiding credit that at least they were ashamed of their wrongdoing.

How many of us who do wrong, know we're wrong, plan to be wrong, are not worried about the consequences of wrong, and have no sense of shame! I don't hear parents saying it very much now, but when I was a child and did wrong, the first thing I heard was, "Shame on you!" You've brought shame to your family. You've brought shame to your God. You've brought shame to yourself. Shame on you! At least these brothers were ashamed of what they had done to their own. Not only were they ashamed, they were willing to admit that they were wrong. They were willing to stand up and say, "I made an error." We'd rather die than say we were wrong. We'd rather lose a leg than admit that our ignorance outdistances our discretion. But I'll tell you what, it takes a strong individual to say he's wrong. It takes a person of character to admit that he made a mistake. At least these brothers had the willingness to admit they were wrong.

But that's not the way you deal with evil. If you're waiting on somebody to be ashamed, you'll be waiting a long time. If you're waiting on somebody to admit error, you'll be waiting a long time.

When Joseph was faced by evildoers in his life, what he said to them was, "Fear not. Don't worry. You don't have any cause for concern. I'm not the one you have to worry about. I don't know whether Daddy said I'm supposed to forgive you or not, but I think you ought to know that I've already forgiven you. You don't have to worry about my taking revenge. You don't have to worry about my trying to get even with you. I know that I've had to deal with evil in my life, but I just wanted to tell you, fear not."

Now, my friends, the reason that Joseph was able to tell his brothers to *fear not* was because he understood what the theme of the book was. Joseph understood that the theme of the book is not Joseph but God.* What Joseph said was, "Am I in the place of God?"

I'm not in the place of God.

I'm not your maker. I'm not your creator.

I'm not responsible for your getting here, I won't be responsible when you're gone.

I'm not your judge and I'm not your jury.

I'm not going to hold the record book when you stand at the bar of judgment.

I'm not the one who will divide the sheep from the goats and the wheat from the tares.

I'm not the one who sits high and looks low.

I'm not in the place of God. You have to see Him for yourself.

He has more justice than any judge. He has more records than any courtroom. He doesn't need any help from me. He's

---

*The reader will understand, of course, the preacher's use of imaginative license. Obviously the Book of Genesis was not available to Joseph. Such license will be detected in many of these sermons and is a part of my preaching style. It is also, I believe, typically a part of the preaching experience within the black idiom.

God all by Himself, and He doesn't need anybody else. I am not in the place of God.

And so I hear Joseph saying, "You know you've really helped me out. You've helped me come to grips with this evil problem. I often wondered how it was that God expected me to be His servant and at the same time I had to deal with this problem of evil all around me. But you see I've discovered that God has a recycling process as far as evil is concerned. He takes it one way, but it comes out another way."

You know what the recycling process is all about. In this modern age they take old tin scrap, an old Coke can, and even though it's empty and all of its contents have been spilled, the laws of sanitation will not permit the tin can to be refilled and reused—you can take an old aluminum can out and throw it in the trash can. But somehow, way out at the dump there's somebody who's gathering up aluminum cans. They take those old cans and melt them down and run them through a refining process and after a while, and by and by, what we throw out one day comes back a brand new can!

Well, God has a recycling process with evil. That's why Joseph said to his brothers, "You thought evil against me; but God meant it unto good!" What you thought would be my bad times, God has a recycling process to turn into my good times.

> What you thought would be my defeat, God has a recycling process to make my victory.
>
> What you thought would be my shame, God has a recycling process to make my success.
>
> What you thought would be my way out, God has a recycling process to make my way up.
>
> What you thought would be my midnight, God has a recycling process to make my morning.
>
> What you thought would have me limping, God has a recycling process to keep me leaping.
>
> What you thought would be my stumbling block, God has a recycling process to make my steppingstones.

You meant evil unto me, but God meant it for good!

Joseph is not the only one who knows how to deal with this problem of evil.

I talked to Job the other night, and Job said, "He shall deliver thee in six troubles: yea, in seven there shall no *evil* touch thee" (Job 5:19).

I talked to David the other night, and David told me, "Yea, though I walk through the valley of the shadow of death, I will fear no *evil*: for thou art with me" (Psalm 23:4).

I went back and asked him again, "David, what do you do when there's evil all around your life?" and David told me to tell you:

> Fret not thyself because of *evil-doers*, neither be thou envious against the workers of iniquity. For they shall soon be cut down like the grass, and wither as the green herb. Trust in the Lord, and do good; so shalt thou dwell in the land, and verily thou shalt be fed (Psalm 37:1–3).

But I wasn't satisfied with that, and I had to run and ask Jesus what to do. Jesus told me to tell you:

> Resist not *evil*: but whosoever shall smite thee on thy right cheek, turn to him the other also. And if any man will sue thee at the law, and take away thy coat, let him have thy cloak also. . . . Love your enemies, bless them that curse you, do good to them that hate you, and pray for them which despitefully use you (Matthew 5:39–40, 44).

In this way alone do we learn to recycle evil.

EPILOGUE

Much to my surprise, "Recycled Evil" was warmly received by many. It is always difficult to measure the reaction of those who hold opposing views, but there was a genuine sense of celebration which seemed to engulf the whole of the church even though, as preacher, I was emotionally drained and spent. My perception was that even though it was a word with sting and bite, it was faithful to the context of Scripture and lifted up a word of ultimate hope even in the presence of the extensive evil I seemed to be experiencing. There remained more than a considerable segment of the congregational population who needed to hear again that God is in control, that hard times don't last, that right will win out in the end.

It is also apparent that even in times of storm, there yet remains a freedom and liberty for the preacher to exercise his craft and calling. Whether in a storm or not, the preacher is always granted the latitude to say a word against sin and evil. Accepted or not, it was my belief that it was a necessary and urgent word which could not be denied.

There was, it appears to me, more than a hint of the forgiving justice of God in the presence of evil. A gospel which proclaims no forgiveness is not the gospel at all—it is a perverted preachment which has no place in the pulpit of Jesus Christ. Basic to the Christian kerygma is that we forgive because of our need to be forgiven. Sin is extensive and includes you and me. "The greatest beauty of Christian doctrine," says Scott Peck,

> is its understanding approach to sin. It is a two-pronged approach. On the one hand, it insists upon our sinful human nature. Any genuine Christian, therefore, will consider himself or herself to be a sinner. . . . On the other hand, Christian doctrine also insists that we are forgiven our sins—at least as long as we experience contrition for them. Fully realizing the extent of our sinfulness, we are likely to feel almost over-whelmed by hopelessness if we do not simultaneously believe in the merciful and forgiving nature of the Christian God. Thus the church, when in its right mind, will also insist that to endlessly dwell on each and every smallest sin one has committed is itself a sin. Since God forgives us, to fail to forgive ourselves is to hold ourselves higher than God—thereby indulging in the sin of a perverted form of pride.[5]

It is important to conclude, then, that the preacher-pastor must be extremely cautious in the identification of evil. Because evil is always dressed in disguise, one must not mistake it for honest opposition and thoughtful, constructive criticism. The church which I serve is congregational in its form of government, which permits and encourages expression of opposing opinions. With charity we must acknowledge that it is possible to be righteously wrong and arrogantly right.

The question before us is not simply one of morals (right or wrong) but one of motive (constructive or destructive). I am beginning to discover that those who wounded me most and whose support I feared completely lost are now seeking to swing the pendulum back to the point of a more wholesome relationship. Grace makes the restoration of these relationships necessary and possible. Paul counsels, "If a man be overtaken in a fault, ye which are spiritual, restore such an one in the spirit of meekness; considering thyself, lest thou also be tempted" (Galatians 6:1).

I would not remain with the church if I did not believe that the preponderant majority of our congregation are people of goodwill and growing faith. The congregation is affected by the power and presence of evil as much as the preacher-pastor. The challenge before us is to minister to the evil in spite of the evil in order that the purpose of God—that what men mean for evil He means for good—might be fulfilled.

It might be accurate to suggest that the sermon itself may have been mistitled. To recyle in one sense means to return to its usage. Evil can never be erased. It bears the seed of its own destruction. The energy which evil requires, however, can be redirected and rechanneled to more productive purposes. When faced by the opposing force of evil, to achieve this redirection may be the greatest challenge faced by the preacher-pastor.

> Though the cause of evil prosper,
> Yet 'tis truth alone is strong;
> Though her portion be the scaffold
> And upon the throne be wrong;
> Yet that scaffold sways the future,
> And, behind the dim unknown,
> Standeth God within the shadow
> Keeping watch above His own.
> James Russell Lowell
> "The Present Crisis"

6

IF IT HAD NOT BEEN FOR THE LORD

PROLOGUE

If it had not been for the Lord on my side,
Tell me where would I be, where would I be?

Some years ago, while sharing Thanksgiving dinner with the family of Dr. T. Garrott Benjamin, of Light of the World Christian Church in Indianapolis, Indiana, we began to discuss candidly the problems we had in common in our congregations. I shared with him a growing uneasiness about the preaching event in my congregation. I felt that there was only nodding assent to what I was preaching and saw little evidence of the power and impact of the gospel in the lives of the congregation to which I preached. His response at once startled and convicted me.

"How much Bible study is going on in your church?" he asked.

We had no systematic program of Bible study beyond what took place in traditional programs like our Sunday school, Vacation Bible School, and the Annual Christian Education Institute. I had to admit that my church was *in many respects* spiritually malnourished, and I knew, intellectually at least, that *kerygma* divorced from *didache* (preaching apart from teaching) was anathema.

My pastoral peer wisely urged me to develop in my people a hunger and thirst for the Word. As pastor I must be personally involved in the teaching ministry of the church. The pastor, I was advised, must give as much time to teaching the Word as preaching the Word. It was important, he said, for the spiritual well-being of the church, and the natural discipline such study provides would bring new substance and depth to all areas of church life.

We were just feeling the first wisps of the storm when I took his suggestions to heart. Since then, our church has been involved in a thoroughgoing renaissance, and Bible study has become the common basis of our church life. The benefit is plain to see, and the dividends of this investment promise far greater productivity.

The experience I have just related is important because it gave me my first insight into why storms come. Storms do not just happen. There are identifiable causes and specific reasons for the storms we face. While we may not be able to avoid all storms, we can certainly take certain precautions. I want to share with you some danger signs of a church headed for a storm. Chief among them is a neglect of the Word in the life of the congregation. The others are a natural outgrowth of that.

What are some of the characteristics of the church heading for a storm?

1. *Churches which do not invest in a serious, responsible, systematic program of Bible study are headed for stormy weather.*

Some contemporary congregations are more concerned about the articles of their constitution than the tenets of the Sermon on the Mount. But according to Baptist doctrine, the Word of God is our "only rule of faith and practice," and we should see to it that our people know it well. We must take seriously the example of Christ who discipled His followers. We must make discipling—the process of firmly grounding students in the lessons of the Master—a top priority in our churches. Any church which spends more time developing the rules of man than it does developing the spiritual mindset that is controlled and committed to biblical principles may already be in a storm and not even know it.

101

2. *Churches which adopt the standards of corporate America as a tool of administration and governance are headed for trouble.*

Churches like my own are blessed by a significant number of corporate and government professionals who bring a wealth of technical knowledge to the work of the church. Used wisely and tempered by the teaching of the Holy Spirit, these skills are a clear asset to the church. Used unwisely, these same tools can introduce confusion into the life of the church. Because of my location in Washington, I often find myself insisting that the church can ill afford to use the government as a model for its ministry. After all, look at the shape the government is in!

The church of our fathers and mothers survived quite well without systems analysis, management audits, or sophisticated electronic databases. These tools, in and of themselves, are not evil and may quite reasonably be used to modernize our ministry. Strict reliance upon them, however, will not suffice. The use of these professional instruments must always be governed and guided by the positive principles clearly enunciated by the Word of God. They may be the tools of ministry but never the end.

3. *Pastors who tailor their preaching to suit their audience are courting disaster.*

Far too many preachers, I fear, use their thirty-minute sermon as a time for a collective ego massage. As my father would put it, they "sugarcoat" the gospel, preferring to say, "I'm okay, you're okay," than to insist with the apostle Paul that "the wages of sin is death." Many among us are far too responsive to the critical comments of our congregations when they say they didn't "like" the sermon. Authentic preaching is not the preacher's product. It is, at its highest and best, a response to the whisperings of the Almighty and a faithful recital of a Word which comes not *from* us, but *through* us. The preacher-pastor who is more concerned about what people think than how people live in response to the demands of the gospel is little more than a leaky vessel in search of a storm.

4. *Churches which do not insist on a compassionate but firm basis of church discipline and decorum are storm-bound.*

Admittedly we are citizens of a commonwealth where the watchword is "anything goes." The church has not remained unaffected by a social order that has moved to the outer limits of permissiveness. Even in the church people feel free to do or say anything. They no longer have a sense of respectful "fear" toward the preacher, the deacon, or any other traditional symbol of authority in the church.

While the fault may be our own, the result has been that members are not at all hesitant to take the church and its pastor to court (witness the rise of malpractice insurance for pastors), expose church affairs to a grateful and laughing media, participate in the formulation of splinter groups bent on molding the church in their own image, and behave in congregational meetings in a manner which produces an offensive stench before the throne of heaven. Unless pastors and church boards have the moral courage and conviction to consistently maintain a Bible based system of church discipline, even to the development of a consistent statement of church decorum and behavior, who knows what hurricanes of hate and hailstorms of hell are on the horizon?

It was just such a spirit of undisciplined independence which occasioned a violent storm in my own church situation. The "infamous" congregational meeting of November 1982 was characterized by such shouts of protest, unwarranted and unfounded accusations, unchristian conduct, overt disrespect for the pastor, and disregard for the church in which they gathered that even now it is difficult to fathom.

At this meeting it became clear that I was the primary target. The attacks were repeated and vicious. Fortunately I was a child of the parsonage, the grandson and son of preachers. Even though I had never been through anything like it before, I knew instinctively that I shouldn't try to defend myself. I knew that I had to wait silently on the guiding hand of God. As long as you believe you are right, there is comfort in knowing that you can "stand still and see the victory that the

Lord is working out for you." I could be confident, the immediate evidence notwithstanding, that "all things work together for good to them that love God, to them who are the called according to his purpose" (Romans 8:28).

Two days later, on Thanksgiving Day 1982, at the height of the storm, it was my task to preach from the same pulpit from which I had presided over the congregational meeting. If that is not preaching in a storm, then, pray tell, what is? Preach I would! The message was unmistakably clear: "Thank You!"

Sermon: THANK YOU!

In every thing give thanks: for this is the will of God in Christ Jesus concerning you (1 Thessalonians 5:18).

It has come to me by reasonably reliable authority that the mark of culture and the stamp of breeding is to be measured by the use of what society calls etiquette. We are characterized either as polite or impolite, rude or refined, by our ability or inability to make the proper use of etiquette. Etiquette says there are certain responses for certain situations. If you ask a favor, it is anticipated that you will preface your plea by the word "Please." If you make an error, you indicate your chagrin with the words "Excuse me." If you interrupt others, either in their conversation or in their activity, it is correct to say, "Pardon me." And if someone does something for you or to you or with you, it is appropriate to say, in response to their kindness, "Thank you." That is the lesson of etiquette.

I bring this lesson to your attention only because we are living in a world that has lost nearly all sense of propriety and order. Very often we don't know what to do, or how to do, or when to do—we just do! People will run over you and never look back to say, "Excuse me." They ask you for the world and expect you to give it and never a word about "Please." There are those who will take you and everything about you for granted and never once say a word about "Thank you." And of all the breeches of etiquette, I don't know of one that cuts more deeply or wounds more openly than the failure of a debtor to say, "Thank you!"

IF IT HAD NOT BEEN FOR THE LORD

You may not have thought of the theological implications of "Thank you," but I believe there is a spiritual dimension to the discipline of saying it. I want to labor with you to show that one of the roots of religion is to be able to join in the litany recital of the simple, uncomplicated, ordinary, everyday words "Thank you!"

*   *   *

You may have all the position that you need, your financial resources may be superior to others' about you, your educational attainments may be far above your peers, but if you don't have enough sense to say, "Much obliged," if you don't have enough learning to say, "Thank you," something is seriously wrong with you.

I must confess that I don't know why, I can't imagine why, a man would not be able to say, "Thank you." As I analyze the inability to say, "Thank you," it may be there are those who are unaware that they ought to say it. They don't ever worry about why things happen or what causes things to be. They're unaware of the obligation to say, "Thank you." That may have been the problem with those ten lepers whom Jesus cleansed. Nine went on their way, and only one came back to say, "Thank You."

Then again, there may be those who are *unable* to say, "Thank you." It's not in their vocabulary. They just have a hard time expressing thanks. But where I come from, if you can't say, "Thank you," that's a reflection on your upbringing and your home training. You may not have any money, but you can have manners. You may be poor, but you can be polite. Everybody ought to learn to say, "Thank you."

Paul was en route to Rome with a layover in Corinth when he wrote his first letter to the young church at Thessalonica. Paul was aware that the church at Thessalonica would have its ups and downs, its risings and its fallings. In order that their faith might be well-founded, in order that their hope might be sustained, Paul sent them a letter about Christian etiquette.

First of all, says Paul, see that none render evil for evil

unto any man. I don't care what you say, you can't live a Christian life on a payback philosophy. Two wrongs never made a right. If somebody does you wrong, you can't go around talking about getting even. "An eye for an eye and a tooth for a tooth" will leave everybody snaggle-toothed and blind. Jesus said, "I have a new commandment, that you love one another." That's good manners.

Secondly, Paul says, "Rejoice!" I don't know about you, but I don't have time for a religion that won't let me rejoice. When I come to church I don't come for foolishness and pettiness. I come to rejoice. I come to praise the holy name of Jesus. And if something is right and it ought to be affirmed, somebody ought to say, "Amen." Some of you sit in service the whole day long, never smile, never pat a foot, never moan, never groan. You don't do anything! I wouldn't go anywhere and sit up for two hours and do nothing. Paul says, "Rejoice!" And you can't rejoice without giving thanks. The psalmist said:

> Make a joyful noise unto the LORD, all ye lands. Serve the LORD with gladness: come before his presence with singing. Know ye that the LORD he is God: it is he that hath made us, and not we ourselves; we are his people, and the sheep of his pasture. Enter into his gates with thanksgiving, and into his courts with praise. Be thankful unto him, and bless his name (Psalm 100:1–4).

That's good manners!

Thirdly, Paul says, "Pray without ceasing!" God knows that if you're a child of the King you will learn how to pray. You had better believe me when I tell you that the devil is always busy. Satan is on the loose. The devil is never satisfied for peace to prevail. The devil is never happy for harmony to be in the house. Satan is the author of confusion, and whenever he can get a foot in, he will. That's why Paul says, "Pray without ceasing." That means don't ever stop praying. Prayer still changes things. You ought to pray for your family. Pray for the one sitting next to you. Pray for the deacons. Pray for the trustees, and God knows, pray for the pastor. And don't forget—*don't forget!*—pray for yourself. That's good manners!

But I wanted to tell you that Paul said, "In everything give thanks." Paul said to that Thessalonian congregation that the zenith of Christian conduct is to be able to say, "Thank you." You see, it's good to take time to thank God for the common things of life.

Thank Him for the clouds.

Thank Him for the rain.

Thank Him for the rolling hills.

Thank Him for the mountains high and the valleys low.

Thank Him for the lakes that flow to the rivers, the rivers that flow to the ocean, and the oceans that flow to the sea.

Thank Him for the sun that marches every morning from the east to the west, chasing darkness with a legion of light.

Thank Him for the moon that follows close behind the sun with a regiment of blackness to form the purple curtain we call night.

Thank Him for the stars that remain in their orbit and for the planets that form a meteoric highway to the heavens.

Thank Him for the grass, and thank Him for the trees.

"In everything give thanks!"

This word says, "In everything . . ." You see, it's easy to give thanks when things are going well. It's mighty convenient to be grateful when things are going great. When all goes well in your world it's awfully nice to say, "Thank you." But Paul says, "In everything . . ."! It is no test of faith, my friends, to say, "Thank you," when the sun is shining. It does not create character when everything you touch turns to gold, when every idea is a stroke of genius, when every morning is the dawn of a day that is better than the day before. That won't make any faith for you. Paul says, "In everything . . ." That means when things go wrong, thank God.

When your world turns upside down, thank Him.

When sickness comes in your house, thank Him.

When death comes and sits on your doorstep, thank Him.

When hard times put you down, when bad times knock you down, and when rough times hold you down, thank Him.

107

When your enemies and your foes come upon you to eat up your flesh, thank Him! Thank Him! Thank Him!

You ought always to thank Him, for God specializes in taking what looks like defeat and turning it to victory. God specializes in taking disaster and turning it to triumph. God specializes in taking the rotten grapes of the wicked and turning them into the sweet wine of the righteous. God specializes in turning what the world means for evil into what He means for good. God specializes in letting one chase a thousand and two put ten thousand to flight. And all you have to do is thank Him.

*   *   *

Paul gave the reason for thanking God in his theology of all-encompassing good. Said the apostle, don't ever forget that "all things work together for good to them that love God." And if somebody does something for you, the only polite thing to do is to say, "Thank you."

You see, my friends, if nothing ever happened to us, God wouldn't have to do anything for us and then we'd never need to say, "Thank You." To say, "Thank You," is an acknowledgment that God can do what He needs to do when He needs to do it. And if I had to call the roll today, I know that Moses is still thanking God that he had a Red Sea that let the children of Israel walk across on dry ground.

Noah is still thanking God for the Flood. That let Noah know that rainbow sign, no more water, the fire next time.

David is still thanking God for Goliath. That taught David how to say, "Though I walk through the valley of the shadow of death, I will fear no evil."

Job is still thanking God because he lost everything he had. That taught Job how to say, "All the days of my appointed time will I wait, till my change come," and "Though . . . skin worms destroy this body, yet in my flesh shall I see God."

Ezekiel is still thanking God for dry bones. His valley let him see God perform orthopedic surgery that let the ankle bone be connected to the leg bone, the leg bone connected to the knee bone, the knee bone connected to the thigh bone, the thigh bone connected to the hip bone, the hip bone connected to the back bone, the back bone connected to the shoulder bone, the shoulder bone connected to the neck bone, the neck bone connected to the head bone, and "O dry bones, hear the word of the Lord."

No matter what your circumstances, you can say, "Thank you!" Sometimes it's awfully hard to thank Him because we don't know why He does what He does. I heard a story the other day of a lady who traveled to England. While there, she stopped in London's finest stores. One day she saw the most beautiful cup she had ever seen. Hurriedly, she went in and bought the cup. Everyday she would take the cup out and admire the cup. She would even talk to the cup and say, "I'm glad that I found you, cup. You're the most beautiful cup that I've ever seen." On her voyage home she tried to keep the cup wrapped up, but she couldn't refrain. She took the cup out and admired its beauty. I see her in my mind's eye as she stretched out in her cabin. Soon she drifted off to sleep, the cup held fast in her hand. And while she slept, she dreamed, and the cup talked back to her.

The cup said, "You know, I'm tired of you telling me how beautiful I am. I'm not what I used to be. I once was nothing but clay and dirt until one day a master craftsman came along and lifted me up out of the mire. I didn't understand it when he beat me and shaped me. I didn't understand it when he put me in the kiln, he put me in an oven hotter than you can imagine. I couldn't imagine why he would paint me and then put me back in the oven to bake me. But you know, I learned to thank that master craftsman because if he had not molded me, I'd be shapeless and without form. If he had not put me in the oven of oppression, I'd have no structural integrity. If he had not put that paint on me, I'd have no color. If he had not put me back in the oven to bake me again, I would fall apart." And so I thank him. I've learned to thank him when I'm beaten, and I thank him when the heat is more than I can bear. I thank him when I'm painted in pain. I've learned in all things, in everything, to give thanks.

Now, as I hurry to my close, let me tell you that as I thought on this message, I wondered how I could say, "Thank you." My mind wandered to that hymn, "O for a thousand tongues to sing my great Redeemer's praise . . ." And it occurred to me that all over the world people of every tongue and nation have learned how to say, "Thank you."

But I don't know any way to say it any better than the old way:

I thank you, Jesus,
I thank you, Lord,
for, you brought me from a mighty, a mighty long way.
Lord, I thank you, Lord, I thank you,
I just thank you all the days of my life. . . .

When I was sick, you healed me.
When I was down, you raised me.
Thank you!

EPILOGUE

Any preacher who is serious about his craft will tell you that the more one learns about preaching the less one knows about it. Preaching is such an awesome and audacious undertaking that one who presumes to "know it all" is already no longer a part of the process.

Perhaps it is because, in my view at least, "Thank you!" is so devoid of any theological profundity or deep critical textual analysis that in the context of this storm it was a word blown in on the winds of the Eternal. Even in spite of the overwhelming cloud of crisis which hung over the congregation, in spite of a new delay which would linger for more than another year, there was a breath of fresh air which occasioned uncommon rejoicing and celebration within the congregational community. To use a phrase common to our religious experience, "the preacher came!"

Who knows what causes the tide to turn or the wind to shift? Jesus told Nicodemus that we don't know where the wind comes from and we don't know where it's going. We only know that something happens. Some may think that it's a matter of a strong leader seizing control of events and effecting dramatic change. I prefer to believe, however, that in this situation something else was at work. Or rather, not something—Somebody! Somebody else had taken up the battle in a manner which would unfold in due season. The psalmist David, who had seen more than a little tragedy in his life, who had been through more storms of opposition than we can imagine, was right:

> If it had not been the LORD who was on our side . . . when men rose up against us: Then they had swallowed us up quick, when their wrath was kindled against us: Then the waters had overwhelmed us, the stream had gone over our soul (Psalm 124:1–4).

> Master, the tempest is raging,
> The billows are tossing high,
> The sky is o'ershadowed with blackness,
> No shelter or help is nigh.

> Carest Thou not that we perish?
> How canst Thou lie asleep
> When each moment so madly is threat'ning
> A grave in the angry deep?

> The winds and the waves will obey Thy will:
> Peace, be still!

> Whether the wrath of the storm-tossed sea,
> Or demons, or men, or whatever it be,
> No water can swallow the ship where lies
> The Master of ocean and earth and skies.
> They all shall sweetly obey Thy will:
> Peace, peace be still!
>
> *Mary A. Baker*

7

THE PREACHER'S FRIEND

PROLOGUE

Three men are my friends
He who hates me, he who loves me,
And he who is indifferent to me.
He who hates me teaches me caution;
He who loves me teaches me tenderness;
He who is indifferent to me teaches me self-reliance.
Three men are my friends!

Unknown

Life without friendship is tragic, yet we know how rare a commodity genuine friendship is. All the more reason then for the preacher—one who is called upon to be a friend to so many—to cultivate for himself wholesome friendships. Any preacher needs friends, but they are especially important to a preacher caught in a storm.

Unfortunately preachers—and I include myself—tend to have fewer friends than most. Perhaps one reason for this is that we are, at core, dreamers. Dreamers, not in the sense of living in a world divorced from reality, but dreamers in the sense of having a concrete vision for what God can do which we nurture in secret.

Somewhere in the soul of every preacher is the belief that he can change the world, or at least his little corner of it. The late Dr. Sandy F. Ray speaks of the dream component of the preacher's personality and cautions that dreamers must be cautious about where and to whom they tell their dreams. It is disconcerting to tell dreams which we cannot sell. . . . Non-dreamers do not buy dreams quickly. . . . Young preachers must observe this carefully and prayerfully. Do not marshal dreams out too early. It is a waste in a dreamless society.[1]

So we tend to keep our dreams to ourselves. But if we have no friend, if we have no one with whom we can share dreams in an atmosphere of acceptance and love, we are indeed tragically caught in the swirl of storm.

During the days of my storm, I perceived myself as a preacher without a friend. It was my belief, though often unspoken and unadmitted, that no one understood me or my dreams and that I could only look forward to weathering the storm without benefit of human friendship. As a result, I isolated and insulated myself from those who could have been my friends, unaware that even then there were so many who were reaching out to me in hope of establishing friendships.

In retrospect, I thought I had no friends primarily because I did not make myself available to be a friend. But my isolation did not make me more secure; in fact it angered me, and I had to deal as well with continuous bouts of depression and anxiety.

As I see it now, a part of my anger was rooted in an overwhelming sense of embarrassment and shame. One discovers by experience that the news of your storm may not be fit copy for the front page of the New York Times. A preacher sees his storm as a national disaster of major proportions and assumes the whole world is watching with critical eyes, not realizing that others far removed may view it only as a minor affair or take no notice at all. In the most violent days of my storm, I believed the eye of every preacher, every church, every denominational leader was turned directly toward me. Consequently, I traveled to local and national church conventions with little, if any, enthusiasm. I found myself avoiding those circumstances where I might be subject to the questions of the curious or the barbs and jibes of those who would be deliberately insensitive and cruel. In so doing, I was avoiding opportunities to share my burden with friends.

Once in the middle of it all, Dr. Gardner Taylor, dean of preachers of the American pulpit, called me at home to give me encouragement. "Henry," he said, "I called to see how you were faring, young man. I have heard, and I am disturbed, and I want you to know that we are praying with you and for you."

A cordial conversation. He offered fatherly advice on ways to neutralize my predicament and assured me of his continuing concern. I was grateful, and remain so to this day, that he should express such caring and kindness.

But I was also incensed—embarrassed is perhaps the better word—that my ministry had brought me to this sad hour. As I had previously determined that the blame for this storm was solely my own, I was embarrassed that news of my difficulty had traveled so far. Embarrassment and shame are the seedbed of isolation. They are not the stuff of which friendships are made.

This friendless moment of my life was exacerbated by the fact that I heard little or nothing at all from those whom I had counted as my friends. Where were they now—those with whom I had studied, those in whose pulpits I had stood and who had stood in mine, those with whom I had traveled to several continents, and those with whom I had shared so many sorrows and joys? Where were they now when I really needed them? Things had gotten too thick. My so-called friends were thinning out—or at least not even aware of my storm!

One friend *did* call to offer advice. He called to say that he had been burdened about me; indeed thinking of me had become so powerful a force that he could not refrain from calling. He called, so he said, to tell me that he had received a direct revelation from the Lord. My curiosity piqued, I was all ears! He told me that the Lord had told him that I should abandon the effort, give up the struggle, and move on in some other as yet undetermined avenue of ministry. I was stunned. If the Lord had a message for me, why did He choose to send it seven hundred miles west? I suspect that the Lord's revelatory process is rather often woefully misappropriated and reported.

I discovered as well in those friendless days that searching for a friend can be an exercise in futility. I had observed with keen intensity the successful ministry of a nationally famous television preacher who had become a role-model for many. I had even attended one of his seminars hoping that I might learn some lesson, gain some insight which would assist me in defusing my explosive situation. Months later he came to Washington. I earnestly wanted to talk with him, to establish a relationship. He had experienced, by his own admission, many difficulties in the pursuit of his own dream. Perhaps we would be able to compare notes, exchange ideas. Surely he would be able to help me.

I arranged through a mutual friend to meet with him privately in his suite. After wading through the entourage, the body guards, I discovered that my private meeting was held in the presence of at least four other anonymous persons. I would not be denied. I told my story, ever mindful of my limitation of fifteen minutes. (How do you tell a story like this in fifteen minutes?)

He broke the silence with his advice. "Abandon ship," he said. "This is not the place, not the time, you will not be able to achieve your goal under these circumstances."

Confused and disheartened, I left that suite as friendless and hopeless as I had entered. I was still in need of a friend, and the storm raged on.

It is important, I think, to share these experiences with the reader because I have been left with the unshakable conviction that in a time of crisis every preacher-pastor needs a friend in whom he may confide his difficulties. My storm experience has left me with insight into the characteristics and qualities that friend must possess:

1. *The preacher's friend must not be a part of the conflict.*

To be sure, a preacher may well have lifelong friends within the congregation. They can be of great encouragement, but they will be too caught up in the storm themselves to bring to the friendship the needed quality of disinterested objectivity. While the preacher's friend must not be a part of the conflict, it is important that this friend have some understanding of the issues. There has to be a base for communication. He should be knowledgable of and sensitive to the internal workings of the church, its political machinery, and its theological underpinnings.

2. *The preacher's friend must not be afraid to tell the truth.*

The preacher in a storm is often unable to discern or appreciate raw truth. The truth hurts. The preacher's friend must therefore be perceptive enough to see through the preacher's defenses and brave enough to be unintimidated by the preacher's stature. He must be willing to declare the truth as he sees it, ask the hard and critical questions the preacher will not or cannot ask of himself, and challenge the premise and the purpose of the preacher's positions and priorities.

3. *The preacher's friend must be able to provide a fresh perspective.*

A fresh perspective is hard to come by in a storm. Unavoidably, every issue assumes life-and-death importance. The real friend is able to ask, "How important is this? If the goal is not achieved, how much less a person are you? How much of your own ego needs are wrapped up in this conflict? How important is this conflict to the continuance of the world? Are you really making 'much ado about nothing'?"

These questions are painful, but the new perspective they bring may well save one's spiritual and psychological health.

4. *The preacher's friend must have the stamina to stick it out.*

Storms are often a long time in coming, and they tend to last a long time. A genuine friend does not expect that a few moments will be sufficient to solve the problem. Indeed, the real problem may never be solved, but it is important to the preacher to have someone who will remain constant and loyal through the whole process. When all else is shifting and moving on the sea of his life, the preacher needs to be assured of someone who will not leave before a new day of hope and self-esteem dawns on the horizon of the preacher's personality.

The Holy Scripture speaks in a telling manner of the need for every man to have a friend. In the siege of storm, the preacher, as well as those to whom he preaches, must be comforted and assured of the availability of the kind of friend to which we have previously referred. The friendship of God and Abraham seemed a fitting example of a lasting friendship, and so I preached "Abraham: God's Friend."*

Sermon: ABRAHAM: GOD'S FRIEND

And the scripture was fulfilled which saith, Abraham believed God, and it was imputed unto him for righteousness: and he was called the Friend of God (James 2:23).

There is within the human personality a profound need which is universally felt but rarely achieved. It is a need which is perpetually sought and continually pursued and yet remains elusive and beyond the grasp of most who seek it. I wanted to discuss this need, this necessity for human growth and development, which when stated in its simplest terms is that everybody needs a friend. This matter seemed of importance when it was suggested by noted authors and psychologists that there are persons who live out the entirety of their lives without a genuine, abiding, authentic friendship.

While I would not want to belabor this point which seems obvious on its face, the reality is that there is perhaps no greater tragedy than to go through life without a friend.

To live without a friend is to reverse John Donne's famous maxim and to establish oneself as an island of self-exile, on an island apart from the main.

Without a friend is to be, like John the Revelator, on an Isle of Patmos far from the crossroads of human interaction.

Without a friend, one faces the bleak reality of life with loneliness as one's only companion and alienation as one's only comrade.

---

*It should be noted here that "Abraham: God's Friend" was part of a continuing series of sermons entitled "Close Encounters." The series proposed to lift up the ways in which various Bible characters had maintained a close and meaningful relationship with God. I found, as well, that series preaching is particularly helpful during a storm as it removes the weekly search for a text and helps one avoid the temptation of retaliatory preaching.

Without a friend, one only knows the tragedy of a personally imposed solitary confinement where the only conversation one hears is the monotony of talking to oneself and the only response one gains to the questions life poses are the result of the limited resources of me, myself, and I.

And so, perhaps it has not come to your consciousness, but I believe we are on safe ground to declare that everybody needs somebody, everybody needs a friend. In your life and in my life, we need somebody who is loving and loyal, somebody who is trusted and true, someone who is willing to be your confidant and loyal counselor. We need somebody who will be devoted in dark hours, present in moments of pain, sympathetic in times of sickness, and nearby when the road gets rough and the hills get hard to climb. Everybody needs a friend!

That's why I wanted to discuss this need for the friendship dynamic in human relationships because, if it is of concern to you as it is to me, I thought I ought to remind you that a good friend is hard to find. Everybody with whom you are friendly is not a friend. Everyone with whom you have a social relationship may not qualify in the category of genuine friendship. That's why somebody told me a long time ago you have to be mighty careful how you choose your friends. Is it not true that "a man is known by the company he keeps"? Whether you like it or not, the world judges you by the quality and the character of the persons you call "friend."

*   *   *

That's why, that's the reason I thought you ought be advised that everybody that claims to be your friend may not be your friend after all. It does not make any difference what the nature of your social or political or biological acquaintance may be. What looks like a friend may not be a friend!

Cain and Abel had the same genetic background, they were brothers by blood and related by common parentage, but the Book says that Cain slew Abel in the field.

Similarly, Jacob and Esau were not only brothers, they

were the twin children of Isaac and Rebecca. But I read here that Jacob got in cahoots with his mother and cheated, deceived, and lied so much that Esau lost his inheritance, and all he got because of this transaction of treachery was a piece of meat and a pot of beans.

You do recall that Samson and Delilah were lovers. Delilah proves that even your lover may not be your friend. Delilah was the one who cut the seven locks of hair on Samson's head and put him into the hands of his enemies.

Job had three so-called friends—one named Eliphaz, one named Bildad, and one named Zophar—but in the time of Job's deepest distress, in the time of his greatest need, all they were able to do was to sit for seven days and never say a word.

Even Jesus discovered that His closest associates could not be counted on. Deacon Peter denied Him, Deacon Thomas doubted Him, and the Treasurer of the Board of Disciples, one Judas Iscariot, sold Him out for thirty pieces of silver and a field of blood.

All this, then, is to substantiate my claim that even though everybody needs a friend, a good friend, a real friend is hard to come by. Husbands and wives can live in the same house, eat the same meals, share the same bed, and still not be friends.

Then again, there are many who have no friends because they do not make themselves available to the friendship transaction. You won't develop an authentic friendship if you're always down in the mouth. You won't experience the sweet communion of friendship and fellowship if you never have anything good to say. The Bible says if you're going to have a friend, you must first be found friendly. You can't expect to have a friend if you don't know how to be a friend.

As I'm on my way, let me remind you that if you have a friend you ought to thank God for it. I've learned to thank God for my friends—those who accept me for what I am and yet don't judge me for what I am not. I thank God for my friends— those who appreciate my strengths and yet stand by me in spite of my weaknesses.

And I may as well tell you, I thank God for my enemies. Those who have drawn close enough to hear my heartbeat the better to know where to thrust their daggers. *I thank God for my enemies*, I tell you, for they are the ones who have taught me how to lean and depend on Jesus. I thank God for my friends and my enemies, but if you have a friend you had better thank God for it.

Now I brought this matter of friendship to your attention in order to facilitate an examination of the most unique friendship of which the Bible speaks. I wanted to take a look at a friendship that James said existed between God and Abraham. Abraham, says James, was called "the Friend of God."

> Moses was the general of the first protest march from slavery to freedom.
>
> Isaiah was God's prophet whose lips were touched by the burning coals of incense from the altar.
>
> Amos was God's agent for justice.
>
> Solomon was God's repository of love and wisdom.
>
> Ezekiel was God's preacher in a cemetery.
>
> Job was God's example of a man who persevered in spite of his predicament of pain.
>
> Nehemiah was God's builder when the walls of Jerusalem had fallen down and the gates had been burned by fire.
>
> Paul was God's molder of the missionary movement.
>
> And David was the apple of His eye.
>
> But only Abraham—no one else in all biblical history (with the possible exception of Moses)—only Abraham was known as "the Friend of God."

And that's why I wanted to ask the question, what does it take to be God's friend? Perhaps you want to know what it was that Abraham and God had that made theirs such a superb friendship. I'd like to know what it was about Abraham that put him in line for such a distinctive designation. Perhaps when you look at your life—as I do when I look at mine— you'd like to know if you might also qualify to be called God's friend.

I know I'm satisfied with God, but I'd like to know if He's satisfied with me. I know He does not really need a friend. He already has the devotion of a Son who sits on His right hand and the comforting presence of the Holy Ghost who sits on His left hand. He really does not need another friend. But I'm curious to discover after being on this Christian journey for more than a quarter of a century, how close am I to reaching Abraham's status as the friend of God? I thought you'd be willing to seek to discover, if you have the time, just what it takes to be so close, so intimate, so valuable, so important as to be called God's friend.

*   *   *

Well, in the first instance, I should imagine that Abraham and God had a solid relationship because God could see that Abraham had his priorities in the right position. You see, *a good friend* isn't always looking to get something. A good friend is willing to take whatever comes along. Do you recall that occasion when Abraham and Lot had a controversy over who would claim the land? Lot took the best land. Lot wanted the most fertile territory. Lot wanted the land with pleasing pastures and flowing meadows.

But Abraham said, "I'll take whatever God gives me. I'm not worried about the land. My priorities are not in property." I hear Abraham saying, "The God I serve told me a long time ago that the earth is His, the sea is His, the cattle are His, the gold is His, the silver is His, and whatever my Friend wants for me will be all right."

You had better hear me today! If you want to be God's friend, the priority must not be in property and it must not be in possessions. Didn't Jesus say, "Seek ye first the kingdom of God and his righteousness, and all these things shall be added unto you"?

*   *   *

Here now, in the second instance, this friendship of God and Abraham was predicated on the fact that they knew how to talk with each other. Not only did they talk with each other,

121

not only did they maintain a lively communication, but they did not always agree with each other. You see, my brothers and my sisters, in order to have a good friend, you don't need somebody that agrees with you all the time, takes your side on every issue, and always thinks your point of view is the best point of view. Good friends can argue and still be on the same side. Good friends can disagree, but still refuse to be disagreeable. Good friends need not always see eye to eye, but they must be willing to listen to what the other has to say.

You do remember that God and Abraham—these good friends—had an argument one day. God looked down and saw the city of Sodom and decided the only thing He could do would be to destroy it. But Abraham objected saying, "Well now, God, have you thought through your decision carefully? Have you examined your alternatives or considered the options that are before you? I know that you are omniscient, and I know I can't tell you anything you don't already know, but before you destroy the city of Sodom, I wanted to ask what would you do if I found fifty righteous men or forty-five or twenty or even one other righteous man in the city?"

And I heard God say, "Abraham, you have a good point. If you find one, I won't destroy the city."

What I'm trying to say is that God and Abraham were good friends because they talked to each other. And if you're going to be the friend of God, you have to talk to Him and He has to talk to you. When you pray it ought not be a one-way conversation. Every now and then you ought to be still and listen for a still, small voice. If you are truly God's friend you can say:

> I come to the garden alone,
> While the dew is still on the roses;
> And the voice I hear, falling on my ear,
> The Son of God discloses.
>
> And He walks with me, and He talks with me,
> And He tells me I am His own;

And the joy we share as we tarry there
None other has ever known.

C. Austin Miles

*   *   *

If there was an element which occasioned the friendship of God and Abraham, it was that God found in Abraham the quality of faithful obedience. When God said, "Go," Abraham did not have any questions. God said, "Abraham there are two things I'm going to do. The first thing I'm going to do is to tell you to get out of your country. Leave your kinsmen and go to a country that I will show you. You will not have a road map. There will be no chart or compass. Just go where I send you." When God tells you to do something, you ought to do it. The old folks often reminded us that "obedience is better than sacrifice." Even though you do not understand and even though the way does not seem clear, I'm satisfied today:

When we walk with the Lord in the light of His Word,
What a glory He sheds on our way!
While we do His good will He abides with us still,
And with all who will trust and obey.

Trust and obey—for there's no other way
To be happy in Jesus but to trust and obey.

John H. Sammis

The second thing God did was to tell him, "Since you've proven to be so faithful, I'm going to change your name. I'm going to alter your identity, I'm going to refashion the manner by which you are known, I'm going to change your name." If you are a child of God and if you are surely God's friend, He will change your name. Jacob had his name changed to Israel. Saul had his name changed to Paul. Simon had his name changed to Peter. Abram had his name changed to Abraham. Sarai had her name changed to Sarah. And if you are God's friend, you ought to be able to say with the slaves of old, "I know I been changed. The angels in heaven done changed my name!"

In the final analysis, God and Abraham found a solid

foundation for their friendship because in their lives both encountered a significant birth experience. I read the birth announcement that said,

RABBI AND MRS. ABRAHAM
ARE PLEASED TO ANNOUNCE
THE BIRTH OF THEIR SON ISAAC

I heard God's birth announcement when He dispatched a legion of angels to herald the news,

UNTO YOU IS BORN THIS DAY
IN THE CITY OF DAVID
A SAVIOUR, WHICH IS CHRIST THE LORD

The significance of the birth of Isaac came to its zenith when God told Abraham to take his only son Isaac up to Mount Moriah and there lay him down on the altar of sacrifice. You should have been there that day when Abraham took his son and laid him on the altar. I heard Isaac say, "I see the altar, and I see the wood, and I know this is the mountain of sacrifice, but where is the lamb?"

Well, it took God forty-two generations to answer Isaac's question, "Where is the lamb?" I know that Abraham asked God, "Why did you let Isaac live when I was ready to offer him in sacrifice?"

But God told Abraham, "I had to let your son live in order to save the nation. I had to let your son live because in Isaac was Jacob and in Jacob was Reuben, Simeon, and Levi. In Jacob was Judah, Zebulun, and Issachar. In Jacob was Dan, Gad, and Asher. And in Jacob was Naphtali and Joseph and Benjamin. I let Isaac live in order to save the nation.

"But, Abraham, My Son died to save the world. My Son died to answer Isaac's question. Where is the lamb? He is the Lamb."

He is the Lamb that takes away the sin of the world. He is the Lamb, He is the dying Lamb. I heard somebody say:

Dear dying Lamb, Thy precious blood
Shall never lose its power,

THE PREACHER'S FRIEND

Till all the ransomed Church of God
Be saved to sin no more.

William Cowper

*　　*　　*

I don't know how you feel about it, but it's a mighty fine thing to have a good friend. I don't want a friend who'll claim to be with me through thick and thin. I want a friend who will go with me to the end. I don't want a friend who will be with me as long as I'm right. I can do all right when I'm right. I want a friend who'll be with me when I'm wrong.

Are you looking for a friend like Naomi and Ruth to say, "Whither thou goest I will go"?

Are you looking for a friend like Aquila and Priscilla to have a church in their house?

Are you looking for a friend like Paul and Silas to sing in the midnight and pray behind prison bars?

Are you looking for a friend like Peter and John to run a foot race to the empty tomb in a deserted garden?

Are you looking for a friend like those two men on the Emmaus Road who told the world, "Did not our hearts burn within us while the man of God talked with us by the way?"

If you're looking for a friend today, I came by to let you know that I've found a Friend who sticks closer than a brother. I've found a Friend who's nearer than breathing and closer than hands and feet.

I've found a Friend:

> Jesus is all the world to me,
> My life, my joy, my all;
> He is my strength from day to day,
> Without Him I would fall.
> When I am sad to Him I go,
> No other one can cheer me so;
> When I am sad He makes me glad—
> He's my friend.
>
> *Will H. Thompson*

125

EPILOGUE

The need for a friend is so critical and important in the life of a storm-bound preacher that it cannot possibly be overemphasized. Unfortunately the preacher's friends cannot be cultivated or located during the seizure of storm. This is all the more reason why the preacher must make a friendship investment in preparation for some unforeseen stormy day. However, the most imminent danger to the friendless preacher is that he become a preacher in hiding. It is too convenient to hide, like Elijah, under a juniper tree of our own fear or in a cave of our own narcissism.

Let me balance these comments, however, by acknowledging that there are many moments when the preacher, for the purposes of maintaining his own sanity, covets moments of solitude. The preacher lives in a glass house. His every move is subject to public scrutiny. He feels naked and exposed, and craves privacy. Richard Bach pinpoints the problem accurately:

> Other people think they know what you are: glamour, sex, money, power, love. It may be a . . . dream which has nothing to do with you, maybe it's something you don't even like, but that's what they think you are. People rush at you from all sides, they think they're going to get these things if they touch you. It's scary, so you build walls around yourself, thick glass walls while you're trying to think, trying to catch your breath. You know who you are inside, but people outside see something different. You can choose to become the image, and let go of who you are, or continue as you are and feel phony when you play the image. . . . Or you can quit![2]

But a preacher also needs to be able to know he has a friend, and that became a particularly important affirmation for me. I did indeed have friends—wife, family, pastoral peers—but they were too close, too loving and emotive to be the kind of friend I sought. Praise God, just in time, I found the mortal friend I so sorely needed in the days of my storm, a friend who did provide the objectivity and the insistence on hard truth, who asked those critical questions and gave me fresh perspective, and who had the courage to see it through.

THE PREACHER'S FRIEND

At yet another level I must acknowledge the presence of countless friends who were there even when I did not know it. The litany of business persons, politicians, lawyers, financiers, preachers, and citizens of the community who spoke a needed word in a time and place beyond my knowing are many. How often it is that the Lord is raising up friends for us that we have never known and will never meet. Unseen hands, unheard conversations, unknown kindnesses by unknown persons are often the way God does His work in His world and ours.

It should also be noted that one of the primary reasons many preachers avoid long-term friendships, especially within their own congregations, is that those friendships often become unwarranted targets of envy, jealousy, and suspicion.

As valuable as the preacher's friend is, I also discovered that I needed something more. I had to become my own friend. Only as I was a friend to myself could I be a friend to others. I discovered as well that I could be free of the tyranny of the expectations which others had of me. I was free to be me. Confident in my own self-acceptance, I felt less threatened by those who did not love me, content in the knowledge that I could accept and love the me inside that nobody knew but me.

But more than this, beyond human friendship, I was able to restore anew a relationship with a Friend who had never left. I found again the joy of my salvation. Where once my hours were "tedious and tasteless," I was now able to "taste and see that the Lord is good." It suddenly made new sense of that time-honored line of an old gospel hymn, "This joy I have, the world didn't give it to me; the world didn't give it and the world can't take it away!"

> There's not a friend like the lowly Jesus—
> No, not one! no, not one!
> None else could heal all our soul's diseases—
> No, not one! no, not one!
>
> Jesus knows all about our struggles,
> He will guide till the day is done;
> There's not a friend like the lowly Jesus—
> No, not one! no, not one!
>
> *Johnson Oatman, Jr.*

8

TRAGEDY OR TRIUMPH?

PROLOGUE

A critical component of the American ethic is an insistence on the importance of winning the game. The winners are the "successful" ones. We celebrate their talents and achievements and promote them to positions of honor in our society. Conversely, we consider losers ineffective, unimaginative, and lacking in the fundamental skills required to make it. We have, in effect, adopted the adage of Vince Lombardi: "Winning isn't everything, it's the only thing!"

Not so the church. We have our winners and losers too. Our winners exult over their victory, and our losers bemoan their loss. But in the church, winning and losing are not as simple as they may at first appear. In any conflict or struggle within the church, winning and losing must always be viewed in the light of the gospel of forgiveness and love. Consequently, winners are well-warned by the gospel not to relish their upper-hand position over much. After all, "the first shall be last, and the last shall be first." Losers who have been defrauded of victory can take comfort in the knowledge that "God is not mocked: for whatsoever a man soweth, that shall he also reap."

If, in the church, we are not so taken with winners and losers, how are we to view conflict with its inevitable tragedies and triumphs? If we're not keeping score, how can we make any sense out of it? The answer is that we start out by affirming an old adage: "It's not whether you win or lose that counts, but how you play the game."

How the church responded to the crisis in its midst will be more important to its continuing life in the long run than who the winners and losers were. Viewed that way, church conflict can even have a positive value. We can see it as a learning experience for both pulpit and pew, and we can seek to gain insights from it that may help the church face future crises.

Such a view is comforting and intellectually stimulating when viewed through the clear lens of a fresh perspective— after the fact. While standing in the storm, however, we desperately want to know one thing: are we going to win or lose? Which will it be for us: triumph or tragedy? Which way will the pendulum swing: toward the depressing sorrow of defeat or toward the exhilarating peaks of victory? At some time or another every preacher comes to that moment when his "kingdom" is weighed in the balance, and he stands in the tenuous twilight of decision, wondering if he or his ministry will be found seriously wanting.

During the time of final delay, somewhere between November 1982 and October 1983, I could not be certain from one day to the next which way the pendulum would swing. Every day, every Sunday, every board meeting was an adventure in the unknown, that nauseating twilight zone between victory and defeat. In this period of ministry, every move was scrutinized, every word critically analyzed, every motive held up to the light of public inspection, and every decision which moved toward reconciliation was revealed to the opposition and rejected, sometimes even before the vote for its passage had been taken.

I learned lessons, though, even in this frustrating period of tension and uncertainty. They are lessons which it might be helpful to review now.

The first lesson I learned was, *Don't give up the ship.* I mentioned earlier that one is not so much made the pastor as one goes through a long and often frustrating process of becoming the pastor. During that process the preacher may be tempted to quit, to give up in defeat. The thought may even come—if only for a moment—of actual physical suicide in preference to the process of delayed homicide through which one is going. Fortunately, the healthy personality will see this effort toward "ultimate escape" as an exercise in "ultimate cowardice" and will abandon out of hand such notions which are antithetical to the principles of the Lord of creation and life. The preacher cannot give up the ship.

Additionally, the preacher-pastor must come to realize that he is not alone in the boat. There are other passengers who are depending upon his steady hand at the helm, and the primary objective of the pilot is not to lose the ship but to land it in the harbor of salvation and safety.

The second and related lesson was that I had to learn *the ethic of endurance.* If I heard it once, I heard it a thousand times, "The pastor is impatient; he must learn to be more patient with the process." Admittedly, patience is a virtue. Unfortunately, in my predicament it was a virtue I often found in short supply. It's sad but true that we pastors have not achieved the perspective of Paul, who could say, "I have learned in whatever state I am, therewith to be content" (Philippians 4:11). Patience and contentment are not often included in a preacher's parcels in a storm situation. But more important than either is endurance.

Endurance says, "I don't like it, but I'll put up with it." Endurance says, "I don't feel no ways tired—I've come too far from where I started from." Endurance says, "My soul may object, but if I make it to glory, I'm willing to spend at least half an hour in hell just to get there!" Endurance is what Rudyard Kipling meant when he said:

> If you can keep your head when all about you
> Are losing theirs and blaming it on you,
> If you can trust yourself when all men doubt you,
> But make allowance for their doubting too; . . .
>
> If you can fill the unforgiving minute
> With sixty seconds' worth of distance run,
> Yours is the Earth and everything that's in it,
> And—which is more—you'll be a Man, my son!

The third lesson was one I had learned years before from my father. I needed only to remember it. *"A lie will die!"* One of the fundamental propositions of M. Scott Peck is that evil always exists in the presence of a lie. But if a lie will die, then evil cannot survive. As my mother, sainted in glory, was fond of saying, "Truth will out!"

My fourth and final lesson is grounded in the biblical insistence that *God still has a remnant*. Within every congregational community there is a "remnant" who will not be deceived or deterred, who have not "bowed the knee to Baal," who have "washed their garments white in the blood of the Lamb," and who will be counted among that number which no man can number who "have come up out of great tribulation." The preacher-pastor may indeed be subject to the insult of evil and the assault of Satan, but God remains nearby His hedge and declares to Satan and his imps, "Behold, he is in thine hand; but save his life" (Job 2:6). In the sure knowledge of the guiding, guarding, and protective hand of God, the storm-tossed preacher may be sure that triumph is implicit in the tragedy. Job said it best, "When he hath tried me, I shall come forth as gold" (Job 23:10).

We have intimated earlier that the prophet Elijah stands through history, not only as chief of the prophets, but as one who learned how to move through the swift and alternating currents of tragedy and triumph. John Claypool, in his book *Glad Reunion*, speaks of the importance of the prophetic insights to be found in Elijah's character.

> Elijah was . . . remarkable because of his profound insight into what was going on about him in history. . . . Prophecy is not so much the ability to see into the future as it is the power to see deeply into present reality. . . . For a person with this gift, foresight is an outgrowth of insight, and this was exactly the case with Elijah; he "saw through" the people of his day with eyes like a spiritual x-ray.[1]

In every real sense of the word, every preacher-pastor who preaches to and through a storm must be given or must cultivate a sense of spiritual x-ray if he is to survive.

Following are three sermons preached at the lowest ebb of my ministry when I could not be certain of the direction of the pendulum. They served not only to define the preacher's predicament, but to illumine what Charles E. Booth, of the Mount Olivet Church in Columbus, Ohio, describes as "The Prophet's Fear." They came at a point of uncertainty and anxiety for both pulpit and pew.

Sermon: WHEN BROOKS DRY UP

> *So he went and did according unto the word of the Lord: for he went and dwelt by the brook Cherith, that is before Jordan. . . . And it came to pass after a while, that the brook dried up, because there had been no rain in the land* (1 Kings 17:5, 7).

I have come to the conclusion, after a season of investigation, that Elijah is a preacher you would have loved. One would not hazard that preachers are the object of affection, but I believe we are on safe ground to make the bold assertion that Elijah is a preacher you would have loved.

You would have loved him because Elijah never showed up very often. Even when he did make his appearance he didn't have much to say. Prophet-preacher that he was, he didn't make his sermons very long. Because of the brevity of his sermons Elijah's quotability was limited. Perhaps the most noteworthy thing Elijah ever said was, "Why halt ye between two opinions? If the Lord be God, follow him, but if Baal then follow him." Elijah was found in one instance sleeping under a juniper tree and in yet another arguing with Ahab and Jezebel over a bogus real estate transaction related to Naboth's vineyard.

So self-effacing was Elijah, the preacher, that he never takes the time to identify himself. We know not when or where he was born. We are not introduced to his parents, or given any details of his growth and development. Elijah had a way of coming in and going out with long intervals in between. Within the biblical narrative his appearance comes with the suddenness of a lightning clap, his prophetic utterances come with the frightening precision of booming thunder, and even when he left he hardly had time to throw off his mantle, give to Elisha a double portion of his spirit, and step on a fiery chariot dispatched to transport him from earth to glory.

History calls Elijah the "chief of the prophets," but Ahab called him the "troubler of Israel." He had the power of healing in his body, and he knew how to pray. So great were his prayers, in fact, that one day he prayed down heaven's fire to burn up the 450 prophets of Baal and their altar. We don't hear very much about Elijah, but Elijah is a prophet you would have loved.

*   *   *

And so I wanted to draw the picture of Elijah's brief prophetic career in bold relief in order to discuss with you a matter which may be of specific concern to you and to me. As you know, Ahab, the henpecked husband of Jezebel, was on the throne of Israel. It was to Ahab that Elijah came and declared a word from the Lord. Said Elijah, "Ahab, as the Lord God of Israel liveth, before whom I stand, there shall not be any dew or rain these years according to my word."

Ahab, don't look now, but drought is about to overtake your domain. I think you ought to know, Ahab, that your cisterns are about to be emptied, there will be no water to irrigate your fields, crops are going to wither, there won't be any grapes on the vine, and the mouths of your people will be parched. My sermon isn't very long, Ahab, but I wanted you to know there will be no water for three years.

It was then that God spoke a word to Elijah. Said He, "Brother Elijah, you're in trouble now. Brother prophet, you've lost your popularity. You had better go down to the brook at Cherith, and I'll send the ravens to bring you bread and meat both morning and evening. And not only that, you can drink of the waters of the brook of Cherith."

Now the Book tells me that something happened in the animal kingdom that delayed the ravens from delivering Elijah's dinner. Evidently the funds had been cut off for the first system of God's meals-on-wheels program. Not only that, but every day Elijah noticed that the flow of the water in the brook began to diminish. What was once a flowing stream slowed to a trickle, and then one morning he went to the water, but the water was no longer there. And that's why I wanted to ask the question, what do you do when brooks dry up?

Quite naturally we understand why there was no water in the land. Ahab and Jezebel had set up the most godless government which the nation had known. Ahab had raised up a temple for Baal, and Jezebel had gathered to herself an army of false prophets. We understand that the arid condition of drought in the physical order was merely symbolic of the drought which had already taken place in the spiritual order of the nation. The nation was dry. Whenever there is no God in government, the nation is dry. Whenever there is no spirit in the social order, the nation is dry. Whenever godless men pursue godless paths and seek to pervert the plans and priorities of God, the nation is dry!

I understand the drought of Ahab and Jezebel, but that explanation does not suffice in the case of Elijah. Elijah said what he said because God told him to say it. Elijah was where he was because that's where God told him to go. And don't you find it strange that he who proclaims the drought becomes the victim of the drought? Since God sent Elijah to the brook, why does Elijah's brook dry up? Or to put the question another way, why does the brook dry up for those who are on the Lord's side? For those who seek to follow His way and proclaim His Word, why does their brook dry up? What I mean is, going to the brook was God's idea in the first place, and I don't quite comprehend why God would sabotage His own plans and programs. I'd like to know what you do when the spigot of the Spirit is shut off? What do you do when the faucet of faith no longer flows? What do you do when the brook dries up?

I assure you I would not want to engage you in irrelevant religious rhetoric. Perhaps in the unfolding of your days you've had the experience of seeing your own brooks dry up. Whenever you lose that which gives meaning and importance to your life, your brook has dried up. Whenever that which you were relying on and counting on and depending on fails to satisfy you, your brook has dried up. Whenever you can no longer find the thing that puts a smile on your face and joy in your soul, your brook has dried up.

TRAGEDY OR TRIUMPH?

When whatever you've invested in fails to give a return and your bank accounts no longer provide the interest they promised, and when all of your assets turn into liabilities, your brook has dried up.

When husbands and wives don't love and relate to each other, and when communication has been shut down and shut off, when the child you gave your life for becomes disruptive and disrespectful and it tears away every day at the strings of your heart, your brook has dried up.

When you come to church Sunday after Sunday and you sing the songs but you don't have any melody in your soul, your prayers have become repetitious and you're just sick and tired of seeing men put on "an outside show for an unfriendly world," and when you come here for some spirit only to find out that Satan is in charge and the Holy Ghost hasn't got a chance, your brook has dried up. And that's why I wanted to ask this question: what do you do when your brook dries up?

Now, in the instance of Elijah, it is important to understand that the brook was *a hiding place*. The brook was for Elijah only temporary housing in an emergency situation. It is not a *holding* place, it was only a *hiding* place. And I just need to tell you that when you try to do God's will, God will provide a hiding place. My Bible tells me that

Moses fled to Midian from the wrath of the Egyptians and hid there for forty years.

David found shelter from the malice of Saul at Engedi.

John the Evangelist was protected from persecution on the Isle of Patmos.

Martin Luther took refuge from his enemies in the castle of Wartburg.

Tyndale, the first translator of the English Bible had to find a hiding place in Marburg, Antwerp, Worms, and Cologne.

Martin Luther King even found a hiding place and the time to catch up on his correspondence when he wrote his most famous letters from a Birmingham jail.

Elijah was given his brook because he needed a hiding place safe from the armies of Ahab and the hordes of Jezebel. And I'll tell you what, when God hides you, you have been hid. If you don't believe me, ask David. I heard David say, "He that dwelleth in the secret place of the most high shall abide under the shadow of the Almighty. . . . He shall cover thee with his feathers, and under his wings shalt thou trust."

The brook is not a holding place, it's just a *hiding* place. But I'd still like to know, what do you do when your brook dries up?

We ought not overlook the fact that while Elijah was at the brook, God arranged for the birds to cooperate with the brook. It says here that God commanded the ravens to feed Elijah in his exile. The raven—symbol of death and disaster. The raven—his silken black body known as the messenger of misery to mankind. Did not Edgar Allan Poe speak of the evil omen of the raven?

> Once upon a midnight dreary, while I pondered, weak and weary,
> Over many a quaint and curious volume of forgotten lore—
> While I nodded, nearly napping, suddenly there came a tapping,
> As of some one gently rapping, rapping at my chamber door.

God now sends a raven to the aid of a frustrated prophet in a dry and ravaged land. But the lesson here is that God is in control of the whole of the created order. If God can't depend on man, He can still depend on the animals.

> Man would not believe Reverend Noah when he told them the rain was on the way. But the animals booked passage on the ark and went up the gangplank two by two.
>
> Balaam was rebuked for his disobedience by the ass on which he was riding.
>
> Jonah disobeyed but God sent a fish to bring him back to prophesy in Nineveh.
>
> Nebuchadnezzar tried to kill Brother Daniel but he did not know that God had already worked out an agreement for leniency with the lion.

He who provides meat for the fowls of the air will make the fowls of the air provide meat for man. If you won't cooperate with God, He'll send a raven to do what you won't do. If you won't line up on the Lord's side, He'll let a raven take your place. God is in charge of men and animals.

David said, "The earth is the LORD's, and the fulness thereof; the world, and they that dwell therein" (Psalm 24:1). The cattle of a thousand hills are His. The sea is His. The birds of the air. The fish of the sea. It all belongs to Him. And when you are in hiding from the Ahabs and the Jezebels of the world, God will send a raven to feed you. But I still want to know, what do you do when your brook dries up?

When your brook dries up, it will force you to acknowledge who it is that provided the brook in the first place. I should imagine that Reverend Elijah had become rather comfortable with the flowing of the brook in his life, so much so that he just expected that the brook would always be there. It is a dangerous thing to take the blessings of God's brooks for granted. Just because you have a babbling brook of self-contentment today doesn't mean that your brook will flow tomorrow.

God doesn't have to send the sun every day, but He does.

God doesn't have to send oxygen for the air we breath every day, but He does.

God doesn't have to send the regulation of our heartbeat every day, but He does.

God doesn't have to give fertility to the soil for seed in the springtime in order to yield its fruitful harvest in the fall, but He does.

God doesn't have to send the water of friends and family, health and wholeness, but He does.

Whatever the brook is in your life, you had better acknowledge that it's not there because you worked for it; your brook's not there because you earned it; your brook's not there because you deserve it. Whatever you have, God gave it to you. The lesson of Elijah is, *you don't miss the water till the well runs dry.*

Whatever the brook is in your life, you had better thank God for it. The Lord giveth and the Lord taketh away. You brought nothing into this world, and it is certain you will carry nothing out. Thank God for your brook. He who made the brook can dry up the brook. But perhaps now even you want to know, after you acknowledge who made the brook, what do you do when brooks dry up?

*   *   *

Well, I don't have much advice to give you on this dry brook situation, but if I could offer a suggestion, I would tell you that when your brook dries up—*don't panic!* A whole lot of folk have seen their brooks dry up, and they've panicked in the process. The economy has turned down, and some prognosticators of the financial future are in a state of panic. Some folk have lost their jobs and are standing in the unemployment line, and now they've panicked. Some have seen their homes destroyed by divorce, and they too have come to panic. But I came to tell you that when your brook dries up, don't panic. You're lying awake at night counting sheep when you ought to be talking with the Shepherd. Don't panic. You can't drown your troubles in a bottle, pills can't pick up the pieces, and you can't chase away your sorrows by always singing the blues.

If Moses had panicked, the children of Israel would still be tending flesh pots in Egypt.

If Joshua had panicked, he would never have walked around Jericho's walls.

If Caleb had panicked, he would have never said, "Let us go up at once and possess it."

If David had panicked, he would never have fought Goliath.

If Shadrach, Meshach, and Abednego had panicked, they would never have walked around in the fiery furnace.

If Job had panicked, he would never have declared, "All the days of my appointed time, I'll wait till my change comes."

TRAGEDY OR TRIUMPH?

If Paul and Silas had panicked, they would never have had a prayer meeting in a Philippian jail.

If Jesus had panicked, He would never have said, "Father, into thy hands I commend my spirit."

Don't panic. Sometimes the brook has to dry up just to let you know that God is still in charge of the water. If you don't believe He's in charge of the water . . .

Ask Moses. Won't God make the water stand back on both sides?

Ask Isaiah. Won't the wilderness break out with water and won't you find streams in the desert?

Ask those newlyweds down at the wedding of Cana. Won't God turn your water into wine?

Ask the man at Bethesda pool. Won't Jesus come by to trouble the water and then tell you to take up your bed and walk?

Ask the woman at the well. Won't Jesus give you living water that wells up into everlasting life?

Ask David where to find new water. "There is a river, the streams whereof shall make glad the city of God."

Ask David. He'll tell you the Shepherd's still able to lead you beside still waters.

God only lets the brook dry up to let you know that He's still in charge of the water.

My story is not over. You still want to know what to do when brooks dry up. When Elijah's brook dried up, God didn't leave him dry: "Pack your bags, Elijah, it's moving time! I want you to go to the village of Zarephath and there you'll find a widow woman. She doesn't have very much. There's no employment in town. She's used up her food stamps. She doesn't have a husband. She's got a little boy to take care of. You'll find her gathering sticks for firewood, and all she has is a handful of meal and a little cruse of oil. But if you'll leave your brook over here, I've got a blessing over there. If you leave your brook on this side, I'll make you some biscuits on the other side. If you leave your misery over here, I'll give you mercy over there."

You want to know why God lets your brook dry up? He's

trying to make sure that you have a testimony. If you never have any dried-up brooks, you can't tell what the Lord has done for you. "I want you to have a testimony, Elijah. I want you to be able to tell men about what the Lord can do." Tell men that the Lord fixed it so you can sing, "How I Got Over. How I Got Over!"

When brooks dry up:

> I've had many tears and sorrows;
> I've had questions for tomorrow;
> There've been times I didn't know right from wrong;
> But in ev'ry situation God gave blessed consolation
> That my trials come to only make me strong. . . .
>
> I thank God for the mountains,
> And I thank Him for the valleys;
> I thank Him for the storms He brought me through;
> For if I'd never had a problem,
> I wouldn't know that He could solve them,
> I'd never know what faith in God could do.
>
> Through it all, Through it all
> Oh I've learned to trust in Jesus,
> I've learned to trust in God.
> Through it all, Through it all
> Oh I've learned to depend upon His Word.
>
> Andraé Crouch

Sermon: ENOUGH IS ENOUGH!*

It is enough; now, O LORD, take away my life; for I am not better than my fathers (1 Kings 19:4).

To be sure, life is always composed of those experiences and encounters which provide both challenge to one's character and the testing of one's spirit. Life's greatest wars are never waged on the plains of mortal combat and physical struggle. Life's greatest wars are fought on the battlefield of the mind. Life's most serious conflict is inner conflict, and the scars of

---

*The author is indebted to Attorney Clayton Jones of Brooklyn, New York, whose insights formed the underlying thesis for this sermon.

war that inflict the most permanent wound and cause the greatest pain are to be found not on the skin, but on the soul.

To be sure, life is not only composed of experiences and encounters; it is also composed of question marks. In every life there are always questions which ought to be asked and which demand an answer. The first question of life is always, "Who am I?" and the second question is like unto it, "What am I living for?" However, when life has been lived to a level of maturity, when one's experiences and encounters have led to some ups and downs, some joy and some sadness, some friends and some enemies, some sunshine and some shadow, some trials and some tribulations, there is yet another question that every man must ask: "How did I get where I am which is so far from where I am supposed to be?"

This matter of life's encounters and questions may begin to gain relevance when viewed against the backdrop of the prophetic career of Elijah. It is to be remembered that Elijah was the prophet who had come to conflict with a king named Ahab and his queen named Jezebel. The godless reign of Ahab and Jezebel had brought the nation to an era of depravity and immorality which had never been equaled in Israel's history.

By various means and methods God had tried to send a message to Ahab and Jezebel. For three years neither rain nor dew fell upon the earth. And still they would not repent. Ahab had been taught a lesson when he tried to execute a quitclaim on Naboth's vineyard. And still he would not repent. Elijah wound up in conflict with the 450 prophets of Baal on Mount Carmel. So powerful was the hand of God on Mount Carmel that fire fell from heaven and burned up the prophets and their altar. And still they would not repent.

It was in the light of Ahab and Jezebel's defeat and in the presence of the victory of Elijah and their God on Mount Carmel that Jezebel sent a word to Elijah. Said she, "Elijah, you've gone too far now. The same thing that you've done to my prophets is the same thing that I'm going to do to you. And the fact of the business is, you don't have but twenty-four hours to live. It will be tomorrow about this same time that I'm going to take your life and give you a dose of your own medicine."

Now, the record says that when Elijah discovered that his life was endangered in a manner that he had never known before, he set out in a hurry from Jezreel in the north to Beersheba in the south. This word goes further to say that when he arrived in Beersheba, he left his servant there and went another day's journey into the wilderness and came and sat down under a juniper tree.

*   *   *

I see a defeated and desolate Elijah sitting under a juniper tree in the solitude of his own sadness.

I see a forlorn Elijah, having sought only to do God's will and to speak a word on His behalf, bathed in the rushing waters of internal turmoil and in the flooding waters of anguish and anxiety.

I see a defeated Elijah suffering the ill effects of a kind of professional prophetic burnout, and I see him experiencing the deepening depression of mental and spiritual aloneness.

I see an Elijah who had come to the point where he had to ask life's most difficult question: How did I get where I am which is so far from where I am supposed to be?

And so, if that question has ever been your question, if you've ever wondered how you got where you are in the unfolding drama of your life, if you have ever known the kind of disturbing depression which draws into question the very meaning of your existence, then perhaps you will think I am correct to tell you that life can be mighty hard when you think you're all alone.

There was Elijah separated from his family, alienated from his friends, and wondering why it seemed as though God had turned His back on him. There was Elijah, who only had worry for his companion and frustration for his only friend.

Little wonder, then, that in his state of mental anxiety and depression, Elijah made an exit to an exile in the wilderness.

The wilderness of solitude

The wilderness of aloneness

The wilderness of sober reflection

The wilderness of internal withdrawal

The wilderness of personal introspection

And I may as well tell you there are only three kinds of people in the world: those who are in the wilderness, those who have just come out of the wilderness, and those who are headed into the wilderness. You may not know it now, but in every life there comes a time for some wilderness duty. You may be riding high today, but there is some wilderness time waiting on you. The Book says that into every life some rain must fall, and it rains upon the just and the unjust.

I have brought all of this to your attention because in the midst of that wilderness experience, God heard a word from Elijah. This word declares that Elijah sat down under a juniper tree and requested for himself that he might die. What Elijah said was, "It is enough. Now, O Lord, take away my life.

"It is enough. I'm tired of struggling with the Ahabs and Jezebels of the world.

"It is enough. I'm weary of wrestling with principalities and powers.

"It is enough. I don't have what it takes to struggle with the forces of iniquity and the regiments of the unrighteous.

"It is enough. I'm tired of walking in the counsel of the ungodly and standing in the way of sinners.

"I've almost starved to death, I've had to be fed by a raven and had to beg biscuits from a little widow woman, I've seen my brook dry up, I've had to fight 450 prophets of Baal when no one else would stand with me. Ahab and Jezebel have got a 'contract' out on my head, and for all my work, I'm out here in a wilderness. I'm out here all by myself. It is enough. And enough is enough!"

*   *   *

Viewed from the perspective of the prophetic vocation, one may well understand Elijah's frustration. A look to the contemporary socio-political arena will reveal disturbing and yet undesirable realities of human history.

The truth is that the most erudite theologian in the history of Christianity was a black man named Augustine. And yet more than sixteen hundred years after Augustine wrote *De Civitate Dei* ("The City of God"), 45 percent of our high school students are dropouts, and 85 percent of black teenagers are unemployed and will not be employed.

The truth is that more than twenty-five years after *Brown* v. *Board of Education* our children still cannot read.

The truth is that 120 years after Lincoln signed the Emancipation Proclamation, black folk are still not free.

The question to be asked of blacks in America today is how long do we sit under the juniper tree of accommodation and conciliation in hiding from the Ahabs and the Jezebels of the world? Shall we like the children of Israel hang our harps on the willow tree and refuse to sing the Lord's song, or is it not the time to tell the oppressor, to tell the agents of immorality, to tell the presiders over godless government, to tell Republicans and Democrats, liberals and conservatives— enough of a thing is enough!

But Elijah's argument was not simply with the social order. Elijah's argument was with God. Now I assure you I do not intend to question the integrity of Elijah's purpose, but there are some matters which seem to me most strange. If you have a moment, I wanted to review this matter, for I hear Elijah saying, "Lord, it is enough. Take away my life."

Now my Bible says that Elijah was already in Jezreel, but when he got ready to tell God to take his life, he told Him in Beersheba. Now I know that Elijah was despondent, but if he just wanted to die he could have stayed in Jezreel. Jezebel would have gladly provided death for him where he was, and he could have saved himself the cost of transportation. And that just leads me to say that everybody that's talking about dying isn't ready to go. You're talking about how bad it is with you, and you complain and moan and groan about how tired you are and how many aches and pains you have. But you're not ready to die. As long as there's breath in your body, you're not ready to die!

I wanted to point this matter to your attention because

144

from Jezreel to Beersheba is over one hundred miles. Elijah ran from Ahab and Jezebel over one hundred miles. Ahab and Jezebel represented the challenge, the risk, the encounter in Elijah's life, but how many of us are running away from our own individual challenges? How many of us are trying to escape a confrontation with some enemy? Elijah ran one hundred miles, but I came to tell you today, don't ever underestimate the traveling power of evil.

You may as well stand still because trouble will follow you. No need to move to another town. No need to send your resumé for another job. No need to search for an alternative lifestyle. No need to join another church; trouble will follow you wherever you go. The hell you run from over here will meet you over there. I understand your disappointment, your despondency, your depression. Enough is enough. But never underestimate the traveling power of evil.

I've been trying to examine the Elijah story very carefully, and I've discovered that Elijah's problem was not Ahab, and not Jezebel, and not the social order. Elijah's problem was Elijah. And if I'm honest in an analysis of my life, the trouble with me is me. And if you're honest in an analysis of your life, the trouble with you is you.

You may as well face the fact that when God gives you an assignment, you had best find yourself doing it. You see, if a doctor has all the equipment to save a life and yet refuses to do it, somebody will charge him with malpractice. And I'm afraid today a whole lot of Christians are not doing what they could be doing and might be charged with malpractice as well. A whole lot of Christians are not serving as they should be serving. Whatever God has told you to do, just do that and leave the rest to Him.

You can't outrun evil. You can't turn back the hand of time. You can't alter the ebb and flow of history. Enough is enough. But there is one thing you can do:

> If you trust and never doubt,
> He will surely bring you out.
> Take your burden to the Lord
> And leave it there.

Now I want to listen carefully to what Elijah's real complaint is. When the Lord caught up with Elijah under his juniper tree, what he said was, "Lord, I am the only one left, everybody else is gone. Nobody else out here is taking up Your cause but me, and they're ready to take my life as well. That's why I say enough is enough, because I'm the only one You've got You can count on."

That's the time I heard God say to Elijah, "You have a rather self-centered brand of religion. I think you ought to know you're not the only fish in the sea. You're important, Elijah, but you're not indispensable. You don't know it, Elijah, but I've got seven thousand besides you who have not bowed their knee to Baal." God still has somebody else to witness for Him besides you.

The Book says that while Elijah lay in his despondent state, God sent an angel to feed him. The angel brought cake and water. I am not surprised by that, because when God wants to communicate He sends an angel.

Jacob was in a hurry, fleeing from the wrath of his brother Esau, stretched out one night, angels ascending and descending.

Isaiah was in the temple, and God tried to get a message through:

In the year that King Uzziah died I saw also the Lord sitting upon a throne, high and lifted up, and his train filled the temple. Above it stood the seraphims: each one had six wings. . . . And one cried unto another, and said, Holy, holy, holy, is the Lord of hosts: the whole earth is full of his glory.

Peter was in jail one night. They had put him in the inner prison, sleeping between two soldiers and bound with chains. But about that time an angel tiptoed in, and his chains fell off.

Paul was on a ship bound for Rome. A storm blew in. He told them, "Be of good cheer. . . There shall be no loss . . . of life. . . . For there stood by me this night the angel of God, whose I am, and whom I serve, saying, Fear not."

But the old folk had a better way of saying it. They said simply, "All night, all day—angels keep watching over me."

God sent His angel to feed Elijah. "You don't have enough for your journey?"

146

"What journey? I'm through. I'm all washed up."

"You're not through yet, Elijah.

"I'm going to send you from where you are to where I want you to be. I'm going to send you from the molehill to the mountain. I'm going to send you from your place to My place. I'm going to send you to Mount Horeb. I'm going to send you where the burning bush is still on fire. I'm going to send you from defeat's degradation to God's revelation. I'm going to send you where you can hear a still, small voice. I'm going to send you from the wilderness to the mountain.

"In the wilderness there is weakness, but on the mountain there is strength. In the wilderness there is loneliness, but on the mountain there is companionship. In the wilderness there is despair, but on the mountain there is hope. In the wilderness there is sorrow, but on the mountain there is joy. In the wilderness there are enemies, but on the mountain there are friends. In the wilderness there is fatigue, but on the mountain there is rest. In the wilderness there is bondage, but on the mountain there is freedom. In the wilderness there is death, but on the mountain there is life. In the wilderness there is sin, but on the mountain there is salvation.

"I'm sending you from the wilderness to the mountain just so I can ask you, 'Tell Me, how did you feel when you came out of the wilderness?'"

*　　*　　*

Well, the last thing I wanted to tell you about Elijah is that it's mighty audacious for any man to tell God when it's enough. What right does Elijah have to say, "It is enough"? We don't have to tell Him.

He knows when our burdens get us down.

He knows when disappointment is all around.

He knows when life caves in.

He knows when brooks run dry.

You don't have to tell God when enough is enough.

147

He knows when to say, "Enough is enough!"

He knows when to say, "You've fought a good fight."

He knows when to say, "Well done!"

> Though the load gets heavy,
> You're never left alone to bear it all.
> Ask for the strength and keep on toiling,
> Tho' the teardrops fall.
>
> You have the joy of this assurance:
> The Heavenly Father will always answer prayer.
> And He knows, yes, He knows,
> Just how much we can bear.

Sermon: WHATEVER HAPPENED TO ELIJAH?

And it came to pass, as they still went on, and talked, that, behold, there appeared a chariot of fire, and horses of fire, and parted them both asunder; and Elijah went up by a whirlwind into heaven (2 Kings 2:11).

There can be little doubt that in the span of prophetic history, the prophet Elijah claims a prominent place. It is accurate to assert that indeed the path and pattern of biblical prophecy would be weakened and sapped of its persuasive power were it not for the presence of Elijah. Elijah the prophet—or, if you will, Elijah the Tishbite—was a man driven by a divine imperative and an eternal summons. He was at once a soldier of the Lord who spoke forcefully to the heresy of heathen gods, a champion of the downtrodden and the dispossessed, and a man for whom miracles seemed to be a part of his makeup.

Elijah is an engaging personality. This inhabitant of Gilead was to be found most often clad only in a leather loincloth and garbed only in a coat made of hair. And I'll be honest with you, I do not know why over the last few days I have been drawn to this ninth century B.C. prophet. I don't know why I've become so enamored with Elijah, the antagonist of Ahab and the nemesis of Jezebel.

He does not have the social awareness of that sycamore tree tender from Tekoa named Amos.

He is not called upon to develop the homiletic preaching skills like that clergyman of the cemetery known as Ezekiel.

He does not possess the tender compassion of that preacher named Hosea who found himself house-bound with a whore.

He does not have any pathos in his preaching, nor is there a tear in his testimony, like unto the prophet Jeremiah.

He never quite manages to engage himself in those flights of spiritual ecstasy, nor is he able to converse with the seraphim and the cherubim, like the prophet Isaiah.

Yet here in my mind stands Elijah the Tishbite. Even this Holy Writing we call the Bible has no book which bears his name, there is not one line which comes from his pen. And yet it is Elijah who is known as the chief of the prophets. Not Amos, not Ezekiel, not Hosea, nor any of the rest. Elijah is the chief of the prophets. And that's why I'm driven to ask the question, "Whatever happened to Elijah?"

In a sense, Elijah is representative of the crisis we face in the matter of biblical understanding. How many personages there are in God's Word about whom we know part of the story, but we don't know the whole story. We read the Bible as a means of finding a word which meets the moment, but if we're really honest we rarely bother to read on to see what the end is.

We don't really know what happened to Nicodemus. All we know is Jesus told him, "You must be born again."

We don't know what happened to John the Revelator. All we know is he was "in the spirit on the Lord's Day."

We don't really know whatever became of Joshua. All we know is he fought the battle of Jericho and the walls came tumbling down.

And I guess it's because I don't think that one ought to let Elijah skip into some anonymous cavern of the subconscious, I just don't think we ought to permit the chief of the prophets to be condemned to some canyon of spiritual nonbeing; it is because every subject ought to have some sense of closure that I wanted to raise this question: "Whatever happened to Elijah?"

Whether you know it or not, Elijah was *somebody*. You do recall, of course, that Jesus inquired of His disciples one day saying, "Whom do men say that I the Son of Man am?" And the response came that "some say you are Elijah. Your behavior has some striking similarities to a man we knew as Elijah. You have a way of raising some questions and speaking to some issues like a man we once knew as Elijah. You have a way of dealing with godless governments in a manner that we haven't seen since Elijah left here."

And that's why—because the disciples were able to make the cross reference from Jesus to Elijah and from Elijah to Jesus—that's why I wanted to ask, "Whatever happened to Elijah?"

*   *   *

Follow, if you please, the drama of the days of Elijah. It is in the unfolding of the Book of Kings that suddenly there stands Elijah with a word from the Lord. By now you know Elijah.

By now you've seen Elijah standing before the people on Mount Carmel, asking, "Why are you limping between two opinions? If God be God, serve him; but if Baal be god, serve him." You've seen Elijah rebuild an altar with twelve stones, one for each of the tribes of Israel, pour water on the altar, and then pray down fire from heaven.

By now you've seen Elijah down by the brook at Cherith where God sent the ravens to feed him day and night. I see him now when heaven dispatched the first meals-on-wheels program, but I also see him when his brook dries up.

By now you've seen Elijah down in the village of Zarephath with a widow woman and her son. You've seen her empty barrel and her diminishing oil. But now the oil flows every day, and her barrel will not run dry.

By now you've seen Elijah talking about that garden Jezebel swindled and murdered for to take away from Naboth. You hear Elijah saying, "Ahab, you've got your garden, but you're not going to grow any flowers. You've got a deed, Ahab, but the deed has blood on it. And, Ahab, the dogs are going to lick up your blood in the same spot where they licked up Naboth's blood, and the dogs are going to eat Jezebel by the wall of Jezreel."

By now you've seen Elijah when one day the widow of Zarephath's son died. Elijah took him to his upstairs apartment, laid him out on his bed, and then stretched out his own body over the dead boy's body. The Book says he prayed over the body of the lad because, you know, prayer can still change things. I don't know what Elijah prayed that day, but I imagine he said something to the effect of "Father, I stretch my hands to thee. No other help I know!"

By now you've seen Elijah hiding under a juniper tree saying, "It is enough now, O Lord. Take away my life, for I am not better than my father." You heard Elijah say, "Enough is enough!" But you also saw Elijah leave the wilderness for the mountain because God was not through with him yet.

By now you've seen the dramatic stages of the life of Elijah. You've seen him in his ups and his downs, his elation and his depression, his victory and his defeat. And by now you ought to be curious, you ought to be interested, you ought to be anxious to discover whatever happened to Elijah.

And so, I want to share with you those things that happened to Elijah. But in order for those events to have meaning, one must first understand the lessons to be gained from Elijah's life. Perhaps if we can discover the meaning of events in Elijah's life, there may be a clue to the meaning of events in our own.

*   *   *

In the first instance, there is a lesson to be learned when Ahab greets Elijah and calls him the "troubler of Israel." "Elijah, you're a troublemaker, you're upsetting the nation, you're disturbing my domain. Elijah, you're the troubler of Israel." Now the lesson is that for a child of God, *names can't hurt you.* If you try to serve the Lord, somebody will call you everything but a child of God. But I learned a long time ago,

"Sticks and stones may break my bones, but words can never hurt me." The old church said it better: "I don't mind people talking about me. This old world is not my home. Every time you tell a lie on me, that's a brick in my brand new home!"

Additionally, the life of Elijah instructs us that just at the time when you think it's all over, *there's something else to be done;* when the time comes in your life when you think you've won the victory, there's another mountain to climb, another river to cross, another assignment to be completed, another enemy to face, another burden to bear, another cross to carry, another heartache to hold, another night to struggle through.

Elijah's life also says that when you think you've run out of power, God has a way of letting you know *you have more strength than you are aware of.* You've got some resources you can rely on. My Bible tells me, "Greater is he that is in you than he that is in the world." My Bible tells me, "He giveth power to the faint; and to them that have no might he increaseth strength. . . . They that wait upon the LORD shall renew their strength; they shall mount up with wings as eagles; they shall run, and not be weary; and they shall walk, and not faint" (Isaiah 40:29, 31).

Well, I guess I ought to tell you that Elijah's life instructs us that when your well runs dry, God is still in charge of the water department. No matter how dark your days, no matter how dismal your night, no matter how bleak your future may be, God is still passing out blessings. Sometime the path of human life can be mighty dry. Sometime the showers of satisfaction are delayed for more than a season. Sometime the soul can lose its spiritual rays. But I'm here to tell you God is still in charge of the water of life.

David said the water of his life had run dry. He had to acknowledge his transgression. His sin was ever before him. He knew he was born in sin and shaped in iniquity, but when his life ran on a dry season, I heard David declare, "Thou preparest a table before me in the presence of mine enemies: thou anointest my head with oil; my cup runneth over." Didn't David say, "I once was young and now I'm old, but no matter how dried up my well got, no matter how many days my brook has run dry, I've never seen the righteous forsaken nor his seed begging bread"?

But I still want to know, whatever happened to Elijah?

I hope you don't mind this little exercise on Elijah. I thought it was important because whatever happened in his life may well happen in my life and in yours.

> I may not be facing 450 prophets of Baal, but I will have some opposition in my life.
>
> I may not be situated by the brook of Cherith, but I will see the time when my well runs dry.
>
> I may never be physically hungry, but I may fall victim to spiritual malnutrition and need to make a visit to a widow's house for some biscuits and some blessing.
>
> I may never own a garden adjacent to the king's palace, but somebody may try to take the flowers from my life and keep me from enjoying the fruits of domestic tranquility.
>
> I may never have to raise anybody from the dead, but I know that death is in my destiny. "It is appointed unto man once to die and after that the judgment."
>
> I may never be ready to give up my life, but I know the day is soon to dawn when I have to sit under the juniper tree of depression and disappointment.

And that's why—because my life may have some striking similarities to Elijah's life—I just wanted to know, whatever happened to Elijah?

Well, the Book says that Elijah gave his mantle to his successor, named Elisha. Not only did he give him his mantle, but it says here he gave him a "double portion of his spirit." And I'm here to tell you, my friends, that on this Christian journey you're going to need a double portion. I don't know about you, but I need:

> A double portion of God's love
>
> A double portion of God's grace
>
> A double portion of God's mercy
>
> A double portion of God's redemption
>
> A double portion of God's salvation

A double portion of God's justification

A double portion of God's Holy Spirit

Not only did Elijah give his mantle to Elisha, but you had better be careful how you read what happened to Elijah. Most often I am told that Elijah went to heaven in a chariot. And I want to go to heaven in a chariot. I want to say right here, "Swing low, sweet chariot, coming for to carry me home." But that's not what the Book says. The Book says, "And Elijah went up by a whirlwind into heaven." God knows that when your time is up, chariots can't get there fast enough.

When the war is over, chariots can't transport you swiftly enough.

When the battle is fought and the victory is won, chariots might not have enough power to get you there.

But God has the whirlwind locked up in the sockets of his jaws. I don't want a chariot. Somebody said:

Lord, lift me up and let me stand
By faith on heaven's tableland;
A higher plane than I have found—
Lord, plant my feet on higher ground.
Johnson Oatman, Jr.

*   *   *

Well, you're still trying to find out what happened to Elijah. I'll tell you what the cynic says. The cynic says that the thing that happened to Elijah is the same thing that happens to all men: he died. But if that's what you think, you just don't know your Bible. The Bible does not say that Elijah ever died. The Lord just took him. Like Enoch, he was just translated. God took him and he was not. Don't ever let anybody tell that I died. No matter how cold this clay is, I will not die. No matter how fine my casket and my hearse, I will not die. No matter how many pallbearers nor how many baskets of flowers, I will not die. I'll just be lifted. I'll be translated. I'll be carried. I'll be changed "in a moment, in the twinkling of an eye." My Bible tells me, "Because I live ye too shall live."

Whatever happened to Elijah? Well, the last time anybody saw Elijah he was in the middle of a summit conference on the Mount of Transfiguration. They saw Elijah talking with Moses and Jesus about the death of Jesus on an old rugged cross on a hill far away. I wish I could have been there one day when the meeting was called to order by the Son of God talking to the great lawgiver and the chief of the prophets. If I had been there that day I would have had to say with Peter, "Lord, it's good for us to be here."

Well, I thought you ought to know that there is a tradition that Elijah is still alive physically and that he's still walking and working on the earth. The Jews believe that one day Elijah will reappear and that he will be the usher who will bring the Messiah for the final redemption of mankind. Every time the Jews circumcise a child, they place a chair in the ceremony in the hope that Elijah will protect the child. The Jews believe that when they celebrate the Passover, they need to pour a cup of wine for Elijah. In other words, the Jews are still waiting on Elijah.

But I tell you today, I'm not waiting on Elijah.

And I don't have to wait for Elijah to bring him on in. I'm waiting today, but I'm waiting on Jesus.

He's God all by Himself, and He doesn't need anybody else.

I'm waiting on Jesus. He's coming with a shout, and He's coming with ten thousand blessings in His hand.

I'm waiting on Jesus. The trump shall resound, and the dead in Christ shall be caught up to meet Him in the air.

I'm waiting on Jesus. The trump shall resound, and the Lord shall descend.

I'm waiting on Jesus, and it doth not yet appear what we shall be, but we know we shall be like Him for we shall see Him as He is.

EPILOGUE

It is a postulate of the pastorate that every preacher preaches to himself and speaks, in the main, to the glaring weaknesses in his own life. It is also a part of our professional parlance to confess that every preacher has only one or two sermons. All the rest are merely textual rearrangements around the same message or theme. The more I read my own sermons, the more convinced I become of the accuracy of this analysis.

The foregoing trinity of sermons most fittingly illustrates both these principles. Taken as a unit, and not as individual offerings, the sermons found the preacher preaching to himself, about himself. It may even be appropriate to suggest that in these instances I found myself seeking to preach my way through and out of my own storm of spiritual starvation, malnutrition, and thirst. To the extent that the works are revelatory of where I happened to be at that particular moment of history, both as pastor and as person, they may have been an attempt to exorcise myself of the arrogance and ineptitude of prophetic fear. Then again, it may merely have been a frustrated attempt at theological shadowboxing in the pulpit!

If it is true, however, that "truth is stranger than fiction," and if it is similarly accurate that the Bible comes to life in our own time, then the manner in which an ancient text mirrors and parallels my own experience is surely an enigma of the first magnitude.

Without question, the storm experience in my life was for me a "dry brook" situation. I had clearly come to the point where "enough was enough," and behind the question, "Whatever happened to Elijah?" was my own implicit question, "Whatever happened to me?"

I am convinced that He who made the brook also dries up the brook and that He who shuts up the waterspouts of heaven also is able to make us lie down in green pastures and lead us beside still waters. As there is justice in His judgment, there is mercy in His chastisement, there is triumph in our tragedy.

> Jesus, Savior, pilot me
> Over life's tempestuous sea;
> Unknown waves before me roll,
> Hiding rock and treach'rous shoal;
> Chart and compass come from Thee—
> Jesus, Savior, pilot me!
> *Edward Hopper*

9

THE STORM IS PASSING OVER

PROLOGUE

WANTED: Honest, trustworthy, positive, highly spiritual pastor to lead large inner-city church. Must be consummate preacher, tireless teacher, willing to visit all sick in ten hospitals and fifteen nursing homes by noon on Tuesdays. Limited support staff. Must attend prayer meetings, preside over boards, supervise all personnel. Must be politically astute to deal with church infrastructure. Must be emotionally well adjusted, spend sufficient time with family, willing to work sixteen hours per day. Organizing, administration, and fundraising skills required. Will not be involved in money management. Candidates will be required to maintain academic currency with theological thought and be actively involved in community affairs. Must not be too liberal, too conservative, or given to extensive evangelism. Moderate salary designed to ensure continuous humility. Must be well dressed, but not flashy. Must be independent, adventuresome, able to initiate and respond creatively to all situations. Must be fearless, flawless, and willing to take all risks. Sermons limited to twenty minutes, modest volume. Subjects must be consistently brilliant, creative, funny, noncontroversial. Applicants must apply in person and in public. Excellent opportunity for self-starter!

Such are the expectations that the church has of the contemporary preacher-pastor. Is it any wonder that storms occur?

I had been on a long journey—a nightmare actually—that began in January of 1979. It was now the winter of 1983 and the long night of agony was not yet over. It appeared that it would never end, that the storm would continue to rage unabated. I could not know—the signs were simply not there—that the storm was passing over.

The passage was almost as violent as the storm. In the late fall of 1983, a letter was circulated which claimed to tell the truth to the already confused and tiring congregation. Some ten days later, another reinforcing letter followed. Both attempted to drive a wedge between pastor and people and to defeat once and for all the majority plan to construct the new church building. Two days after the publication of this latest missive, a regularly scheduled church meeting was held.

The air was tense. All six hundred seats were filled. An overflow crowd packed the back and lined the side walls. The meeting droned on, much as previous meetings had, but something was different. There was a different mood, a change in the wind.

For months rumors of my dismissal had surfaced and abated. It was clear by now that I—not the new building—was the issue. Those who had opposed the construction (in defiance of continuous and repeated majority votes by the congregation) saw themselves as saving the congregation from me and even hinted that they would drop their opposition once I was gone. The word was out: "The building will never go up as long as Hicks is pastor."

I was aware of the threatened move for my ouster, so it should not have surprised me when it came. But it did anyway. I was stunned and disappointed. Disappointed, but not devastated! On the heels of the shock of surprise came a warm, confident assurance which whispered, "Be still, my soul—the Lord is on thy side."

It started when an old woman rose slowly to her feet. The weight of years seemed to burden her stance. The etched marks of time were clearly drawn across her forehead. The atmosphere in the room changed. There was a sudden but noticeable departure of those who knew the text of her speech and would be expected to support her cause. In the closing moments of the night they left the room. Though I knew her name, she became an anonymous entity, the representative of the opposing forces. I felt no bitterness, no anger toward her, only pity that one who should be getting her garments fit for glory could be duped by others into doing such an ignominious chore.

She spoke with a firmness and strength of diction which belied her years, "Mr. Moderator, I have never known this church, in all my years, to be so divided by controversy. Therefore, I move that in thirty days this church be called to meet for the purpose of declaring the pulpit of the Metropolitan Baptist Church vacant."

A hush fell over the room followed by quiet murmurings.

Then another spoke. "Brother Moderator, I second the motion."

Yet another woman spoke out. "What are we doing here? You can't put the pastor out. The church can't do that to a Baptist preacher. We called this man as our pastor, and we elected him for life!"

Shouts of approval. Groans of disapproval.

Then another voice could be heard. A long impassioned plea, a call for reason and restoration of Christian conduct. All needed to ask for forgiveness. Without warning, she sang,

> If I have wounded any soul today,
> If I have caused one foot to go astray,
> If I have walked in my own willful way
> Dear Lord, forgive!
>
> Charles Gabriel

An elderly gentleman rose to speak. "Brother Pastor, I move this meeting be adjourned!"

The decision was now placed squarely on my shoulders. It appeared my choice was tragedy or triumph. In reality the choice was between standing in strength or running in fear. Perhaps this was what the controversy was really all about. A second choice for the church to call or not to call, to choose again their chosen leader. My words at this juncture of the storm would be the most important words of my ministry among them.

"Thank you, my brother. I appreciate your motion, and I understand its purpose. It is indeed a noble motion and I am grateful for your care for me. Nevertheless, let it never be said that I left here tonight unwilling to face the challenge. If this is the will of the church, then so be it. I prefer to stand tonight, however, in the power of the One whom I represent. Therefore, I declare your motion to adjourn out of order, and the chair will put the motion to the church. All in favor of a meeting to be called for the purpose of vacating the pulpit, please rise. . . . All opposed, please rise. The chair declares that the motion fails."

On this night there was an audible sigh of relief in the soul of the church! It was not a minor victory, not a split vote. The majority was overwhelming. I knew now that the storm was passing over.

It cleared faster than I could have imagined. Within the passing of a few hours I was pastoring a new congregation. The divided congregation I had pastored for the past three years seemed to fade away, to be replaced as suddenly by the original church to which I had been called and for which I had developed such fondness and affection and love. We became pastor and people again, the marriage reconfirmed by the storm!

Within two months the titular leaders of the opposition resigned many of their positions. The church replaced them immediately and without debate. What had been sensed by a few was now clearly seen by all. Both the evil and the lie were exposed for all to see. The issue was not the one-hundred-year-old building, not the nature of the proposed bank loans, not the organizational structure of the church, not the financial integrity of its officers, nor the ability of the people to give the needed resources for construction. The issue was not even simply the pastor. It was the very nature and the power of pastoral leadership now and for years to come, no matter what the name of the person holding the pastoral office.

It is clear to me now that I was involved in a classic power struggle within the church. All of the issues which surfaced— constitutional changes, financial investigations, historic landmarks, the quality of loan packages—had little to do with the real problem, the problem of power—where it would be centered, how it would be used, and who would be in the driver's seat.

Think of it! I had come to this church as the fifth pastor in nearly six score years! The years alone were a testimony to the legacy of strong and continuous leadership in this congregation. The power struggle ensued primarily, I believe, because of a rising number of persons who did not want to see the maintenance of this legacy of leadership.

Edward B. Bratcher, in his book *The Walk-on-Water Syndrome,* has suggested that power struggles are nothing new for this church or for any church.

> Power struggles will always be present where two or more are gathered together. The parish is a natural setting for power struggles. The primary reason for this is that power structures are seldom clearly defined or identified in a church. Moreover, there are formal and informal power structures in a church.[1]

It is precisely because there are "formal and informal" power structures in the church, particularly the black church, that the storms appear and are so violent and intense. There is within the black church a whole layer of leadership which is unseen and never casts a ballot in the meeting of the board, but which has influence and power and is always completely informed of every action taken by the board or the pastor. This informal level of leadership runs on the hind's feet of rumor, in hallway exchanges of information, and through downright gossip. In all too many churches the real decisions are made through this informal "grapevine" rather than by the formal structures of church administration.

Bratcher's description of how such informal groups seize and hold power fits my own observations.

> A far more dangerous and destructive power struggle comes when members, either because of their affluence or length of membership in the church, believe that they have the God-given right to exercise power. That is, power is seized on the basis of their understanding of themselves, not as the result of the delegation by the congregation.[2]

Bratcher goes on to suggest that the preacher-pastor must not bow down or become subservient to this kind of "hold-the-church-hostage-to-my-pocketbook-or-my-office" mentality.

> When confronted with a power struggle which involves the usurpation of his delegated powers, the minister must be prepared to take a stand and avoid the takeover by those who seek to take power into their own hands.[3]

Sometimes pastors deliberately "create" storms as a means of affirming and validating their "hold" and "power" or, sensing a "false peace" in the church, they may seek to precipitate a storm that seems inevitable as a way of controlling its advent. Such was not the case in my own situation. However it comes about, if conflict continues and the issue of power remains unresolved, the results are devastating to the life of the church.

If any principle of storm reduction can be gained from this experience, it may be this: there is no substitute for identifying the problem quickly and positively and meeting it head-on. To fear, to avoid, or to delay confrontation is to give the storm needed headwinds to sustain its rage. This is a lesson one cannot learn while just living through the storm. I had to endure the storm first. Only then could I look back and recognize the force of its logic.

On January 24, 1984, three months after the congregation's meeting, construction began. To God be the glory!

With the passing of the storm, preaching begins to accentuate celebration. Not a victory celebration, but a celebration of God's sure presence in the storm and His final deliverance from its dangers.

Sermon: ALL NIGHT LONG

> *And the LORD caused the sea to go back by a strong east wind all that night* (Exodus 14:21).

The purpose of the priority of this time of sharing together is to assure you that the redemptive hand of God is still operative in human history. I wanted for a moment to share with you what every child of God ought to know—that God is still on the throne and, whether you know it or not, He's still got the whole world in His hands. I wanted to share a thought or two with you, if you don't mind, on this idea of God's action, God's involvement, God's personal, hands-on experience with the human condition. And even though no doubt you've known this—and I'm sure you've learned it in your Bible class, and I am convinced you are already acquainted with this concept—nevertheless, if you have a moment I just wanted to reassert, reaffirm this idea that God has the power to alter men, nations, and nature.

Some have power, but God has *all* power. Not only has He *had* power in the past; not only will He *have* power in the future; but I wanted to tell you He *has* power right now. And that's why I wanted to open this matter up for mental investigation and spiritual scrutiny and for theological dialogue, to see if we could not discover for ourselves God's redemptive hand in human history.

This idea of God's redemptive power is nowhere more clearly to be seen than in the second book of the Pentateuch, commonly called the Exodus. Therefore, by way of refreshing your memory, let me remind you that the children of Israel had been in Egypt and had suffered there in bondage for more than four hundred years. The Egyptians, as you know, were hard taskmasters, requiring the Israelites to make bricks without straw and mortar without clay.

However, they tell me that God's redemptive hand could be seen in this matter when, near the Egyptian capital of Memphis, a child Moses was born. To be sure, his only bassinet was in the bulrushes, and his only bath was the waters of the Nile. I know you know Moses, but I thought I ought to remind you that even though his adoption papers called him an Egyptian prince, there was yet some blood running in his veins that wouldn't let him forget where he came from. You ought not forget Moses, for although he had a stuttering, stammering tongue, somehow he had a sense of justice in his soul. It was this Moses, this sensitive spirit, that God touched one day and said, "Go down, Moses, tell Pharaoh to let My people go."

Now this Word says that the children of Israel, led by Moses, left Egypt with at best some rather hastily made travel arrangements and with no provision for mid-route accommodations at all. No doubt somebody inquired, "Moses, how do you know where you're going?" To which Moses replied, "I've got an arrangement with the Lord. What He said was, 'If you go, I'll go with you. And if you open your mouth, I'll speak for you.' "

It was not long, however, before Moses was faced with a circumstance that bore the stamp of disaster and the signature of death. Pharaoh's heart had hardened, and he and his finest chariots and fastest horses were coming quickly behind them. There were mountains on either side, and with Pharaoh behind him, only the Red Sea was before him. Some scholars are of the opinion that when Moses stood before the Red Sea, he was at the arm of the Indian Ocean and the Gulf of Aden, which separates Africa from Arabia. The Red Sea is 1,200 miles in length and from 130 to 250 miles wide and is over 7,200 feet deep. Its surface temperature averages 80 degrees Fahrenheit. When Moses stood before the Red Sea, it was before a significant body of water.

And I brought this to your attention primarily because it was in the context of Moses, with Pharaoh behind him and the Red Sea before him, that the redemptive hand of God became operative in human history. The Exodus writer assures us that "The LORD caused the sea to go back by a strong east wind all that night." In other words, whenever there is an enemy behind you and death before you, God is involved; God is interested, God is operative, God has His systems turned on and tuned in. Whenever the child of God is in danger, God is at work all night long.

And so I became interested when I discovered that this Word says God was at work all night, all through the night, from sundown to sunup. God is at work all night long.

God works in the night when a chill falls over the earth.

God works when the birds hush their singing and only the crickets compose a nocturnal symphony.

In the night, God works when the moon has made its majestic march to its appointed throne, gleaming against the black curtain of creation.

In the night, God works when the dew has kissed the ground, when the hoot owl takes his post, and all other animals have found their way to their dens and caves.

God works in the night.

In the night when, says the poet, it is "black as a pit from pole to pole."

In the night when it seems that those who are sick get sicker.

In the night when it seems that death does its dirtiest deeds.

In the night when our fears are at their height, when our anxieties know new levels, when our despair deepens, when our destiny is undetermined, and when our future is unsure, God works.

Not part of the night, not some of the night, but all night long.

And so I wanted to share with you a few thoughts on God's redemptive work, and there just seemed to be a few concepts, a few germinal seeds, a few thematic threads that perhaps we could take a moment to examine.

*   *   *

I've been looking at this Exodus story a long time, but I believe it suggests to us that revolutionary religion is a dangerous thing. When Moses said, "Leave your flesh pots in Egypt and tear down your tents around Pharaoh's palace," he was tampering with tradition. When Moses suggested, "Let's leave the foothills of the Pharaohs and the plains around the pyramids," Moses was challenging convention. After four hundred years, there is an acceptable way of doing things. After four hundred years, there is a social order here. You can't change the regiments of religion overnight. You can't unravel the ecclesiastical power structure that is wedded to the status quo in a moment.

The regiments of religious piety are always quick to tell you, "Boy, we were in this church before you were born."

That's why when they found themselves with Pharaoh behind them and the water before them they said, "Moses, what's wrong with you? Didn't we have graves in Egypt? We didn't have to come out here to die. We could have stayed where we were and had turmoil. We could have stayed where we were and had hard trials." Revolutionary religion is dangerous. Revolutionary religion will bring us enemies and foes all around. But I came here to tell you today, God works all night long.

And I may as well be honest with you today. I need to tell you that Pharaoh is still on your trail. Every time America starts up a war anywhere in the world, Pharaoh is on your trail. Every time the White House says there is no hunger in America, Pharaoh is on your trail.

> And the sea is deep. Unemployment lines are getting longer.
>
> The sea is deep. Welfare lines are getting longer.
>
> The sea is deep. Our children are not being educated as they ought.
>
> The sea is deep. There is more racism in America today than when Martin Luther King first had a dream.
>
> The sea is deep. There are more segregated schools now than there were when the Supreme Court handed down *Brown* v. *Board of Education.*
>
> The sea is deep.

And so I am convinced that revolutionary religion is dangerous. But on the other hand, a religion that is not revolutionary is equally dangerous. You see, there are some things that history demands. Just consider, if you have a moment, what would have happened if Israel had not left Egypt.

> If Israel had not left Egypt, all history would have said is that there lived some slaves who satisfied themselves with the building of pyramids.
>
> If Israel had not left Egypt, the report of history would have been, there were some slaves who wound up worshiping the idol gods of the Pharaohs.

166

If Israel had not left Egypt, the chronicle of time would testify there was a people who preferred the indignity of slavery to the sunlight of freedom.

If black America had not rebelled against segregation in this land, history would have counted us a people content to live on the plantations of cowardice and shame.

If seven children had not marched to the steps of Central High, history would have been written that here was a people satisfied to do nothing and know nothing.

If Rosa Parks had not refused to move her seat, history would say there lived a woman willing to accommodate herself to life in the back of the bus.

If Martin Luther King had not stood up to the Bull Connors, the Jim Clarkes, and the George Wallaces of the world, history would have said there lived a people with no sense of pride, no sense of heritage, and willing to be slaves for the rest of their lives.

But I'll tell you what, when the Red Sea is before you and Pharaoh is behind you, somebody has to say, "I ain't goin' let nobody turn me around."

When mystics are chasing you and indignity is meeting you, somebody has to say, "Before I'll be a slave, I'll be buried in my grave."

And the record is clear. I don't care how many chariots Pharaoh may have, and I don't care how deep the sea may be, if faith steps out and takes courage by the hand, if determination stands up and pulls up conviction with it, if belief jumps up and holds onto resolution, if commitment wakes up and puts on the garment of sanctified religion, the victory is assured because God is working all night long.

And so because revolutionary religion is dangerous and the reverse is equally so, I wanted to share with you this notion that God is working, God's redemptive hand is operative in human history. And yet, in this process I wanted to ask the question, why does the sea enter in the first place? After all, Moses told the children of Israel only what God told him. Israel would not have been in this predicament were it not that God told him to speak to the children of Israel that they go forward. And I'd like to know—if they left Egypt on an act of obedience, and if they were where they were as a result of divine direction—why must they now face a sea? Or, to put the question another way, why do you have to have seas in your life? You love the Lord, you try to live right, you bring your tithes and offerings, you sing in the choir, you try to treat everybody right—so why do you have a sea?

Why do you have hard trials?

Why do you have tribulations on every hand?

Why do enemies gather round to bring you down?

Why do you have heartaches and pains?

Why do you have a sea in your life?

Well, there are two reasons for the seas of your life. I wanted to suggest that the first reason we have seas in our lives is because at times God has to humble us to use us. When things are going well for you it's mighty easy to get beside yourself. When you have a lot of money in the bank it's mighty easy to think you have the world by the tail.

When your church is going well, it's easy to be a pompous preacher and a pride-pumped prophet.

That's why the Book says, "Do not think more highly of yourself than you ought to think." Sometimes God has to humble us to use us. I might as well tell you, don't get too proud, don't get too haughty, don't put your airs back on, don't get on your high horse.

If the Lord has been good to you, if the Lord has brought you out with a high hand, if the Lord has made a way when there was no way, your song ought to be:

> Search me, Lord,
> Shine a little light from heaven on my soul;
> If you find anything that shouldn't be,
> Take it out and rescue me;
> I want to be right.
>
> I want to be saved;
> I want to be whole.

And I wanted to tell you that the second reason why God puts a sea in your life is not only to humble you, but to teach Satan a lesson. This Book says that God hardened Pharaoh's heart. In other words, God knew what He was doing when He did it. Not only that, He said that He did it "in order that Pharaoh would know that I am the Lord. I want Pharaoh to know. I want the chariots to know. I want the horses to know I am the Lord."

I don't care what you say, Satan can have his way only so long. God has a lesson to teach. "Vengeance is mine, saith the LORD." God says, "I'm still in charge here."

Wickedness can only reign for a while. Evil sits on a temporary throne, and wrong has no permanent station.

There is a God, and He still makes wrong right.

There is a God who takes what the world means for evil and transposes it to what He means for good.

There is a God. He still gives truth power over lies.

There is a God. He still gives power to the faint, and to them that have no might He increases strength.

There is a God. "The wheels of the gods grind slow, but they grind exceedingly fine."

There is a God. He sits high and looks low.

There is a God. He still raises up friends for you.

There is a God. He still makes a table before you in the presence of your enemies and makes your enemies your footstool.

Don't worry about your sea. Satan is just learning his lesson. You don't have to fret about the sea, I tell you. No need to toss and turn. No need to pace a hole in your carpet. No need to worry if the enemy is gaining on you while you're asleep wondering if you're going to make it. All the while God is holding back the water, and He holds it all night long.

*   *   *

Well, men are always trying to second-guess God. There are those who will not believe that God has redemptive power over human history. Scholars are still arguing about how the children of Israel crossed the Red Sea. Some scholars say they started at Ramses and went to Succoth and then journeyed southward and crossed on the west side of the Bitter Lakes, or the Sea of Reeds, or the Gulf of Suez. Still others say they crossed the Pelusaic arm of the Nile, from there to Succoth, then on to Lake Timsah, and crossed either at the northern or southern end. Still another theory says they first made march from Ramses to Etham, and then turned northward to the sea, going up to Lake Bardawil to a narrow strip of land which separates the lake from the Mediterranean Sea.

I don't know how they made their way to the Red Sea. I do know that my Bible tells me that an angel of the Lord went before them, and when Pharaoh got too close, the angel that was in front went around and got behind so it was darkness to the Egyptians, but it was to the children of Israel a light by night.

His power defends me.

His faithfulness abides with me.

His holiness washes me.

His justice justifies me.

His kindness keeps me.

His mercy molds me.

His truth marches with me.

His Word hides me.

All night long.

Sermon: WHEN GLORY COMES!

Then a cloud covered the tent of the congregation, and the glory of the Lord filled the tabernacle (Exodus 40:34).

There are certain words in the arena of religious language which are by their nature somewhat vague, perhaps obtuse and oblique, but certainly difficult in terms of precision in definition. The great doctrinal themes of the church—sin and salvation, righteousness and redemption, justification and purification—all are words (or, if you will, concepts and ideas) which even though they fall freely from our lips, we spend the whole of our spiritual journey pursuing and never come to a full understanding of the word within the Word.

Such is the case with the concept of glory. The word *glory* is a part of our spiritual vocabulary, and it is a word that is primary in our hymns and our praise. And yet, for all the commonality of its usage, *glory* somehow defies its own definition.

To speak of glory is to speak of God and the heavens which are His habitation. The psalmist says the heavens are telling, the heavens declare the glory of God.

To speak of glory is to use a word that in its multiple ways denotes honor and radiance, pomp and power, exaltation of splendor, worth, wealth, substance, and dignity.

Indeed, what the Hebrew knew as *kabod*, the Greek translated *doxa*. *Doxa tuu* is the Greek root of what we call doxology and that's why—because *doxa* is so all-inclusive and comprehensive and extends even to the trinitarian manifestation of the Eternal—we say, "Glory be to the Father and to the Son and to the Holy Ghost."

Even as we enter this dialogue on glory, I am reminded that when considering the concept, Charles Spurgeon suggested that "the best a man can do when speaking of glory is stuttering and stammering." And yet, at the same time, I wanted to share a word with you on this idea, this notion, this concept of glory. As I've been considering the work of the church, and as I've been giving thought to the whole idea of the redeemed community, and as I've been pondering what it is that sustains and supports and strengthens the twice-born, blood-bought sons and daughters of God, I thought it might be of value to take a look at glory.

*   *   *

This whole matter came rather forcefully to my attention while reading in the last chapter of the Book of Exodus. Israel, as you know, had now come nearly to the end of her journey.

Forty years ago at the urging of an old man named Moses, Israel had forsaken the fields and flesh pots of Pharaoh in search of freedom and a land that flowed with "milk and honey."

While on this journey, Israel had constructed a tabernacle, a tabernacle built according to the specifications of one who is the Chief Architect. A tabernacle drawn on heaven's drawing board and designed as a place where God Himself would dwell. A tabernacle—not a temple made of mortar and stone, but a portable sanctuary. Men could carry it on their shoulders. A tabernacle—not to be compared with the great cathedrals of the world. This was not St. Paul's of London. This was not St. Peter's of Rome. This was not Notre Dame of Paris. It was not constructed of the elegant marble of the Roman Forum. It did not have a dome of gold such as would be found on Herod's temple in Jerusalem. It would not have the elegance of the Egyptian pyramids or the haunting grace of the Sphinx of Giza. It was just a handmade, temporary tabernacle.

But for all the things it was not, it was God's dwelling place. The Book says that when the journey was almost over, when the march had come to its end, "A cloud covered the tent of the congregation, and the glory of the LORD filled the tabernacle."

And so if you have a moment, I wanted to discuss this matter with you. I had hoped we might be able to talk about the glory of the church and the glory of the Lord with a view toward discovering just what really does happen when glory comes.

I ought to rather quickly confess that I do have some difficulty, some apprehension and trepidation, in discussing the glory of the church. For you see, the church is not very high today on the list of relevant institutions. The church was intended to be a holy nation. The church was designed to be a royal priesthood. I'm concerned about the church because it may be that we have become so interested in art that the church has become no more than an ecclesiastical antique shop.

I can't help but tell you the church is in trouble today.

George F. McLeod has suggested that the real tragedy of the church is that while the church of the first century was persecuted, nobody wants to persecute the church today because it hasn't done anything worthy of persecution. And if you don't think the church is in trouble today, if you don't think that the church is in a crisis today, just consider the kind of church member you are, just consider your allegiance, your loyalty, your tithes and offerings. The church is in trouble.

Quite to the contrary, however, the fact of the trouble and tribulation facing the church is perhaps the most vocal testimony to the hovering presence of the Holy. There is a cloud that comes over the church and declares no matter what, "I will be with you." Perhaps the question which ought be asked is, if it had not been for the Lord, where would the church be today?

> History says that nations have endured evolution and kingdoms have been decimated by decay, and yet the church survives.
>
> Sociology says that civilizations and cultures have undergone radical alteration and profound systems of change, and yet the church survives.
>
> Political history says that all along the journey we've been wrestling against principalities and powers, against spiritual wickedness in high places, and yet the church survives.
>
> Philosophies tell us that many men have offered new theories and new belief systems and new self-help efforts at individual diagnosis, but nobody has yet surpassed the timeless teaching of a barefoot, itinerant preacher from Palestine. The church survives.

Only the Lord could take the illiterate sons and daughters of slavery and teach them to memorize Scripture they could not read; only the Lord could take those living in holy huddles that started out in warehouses and living rooms and kiss them with a divine blessing that turned lean-tos into temples and shanties into sanctuaries.

Only the Lord could let us live through an era of unprecedented religious history where Reverend Ike has insulted us, Jerry Falwell has demeaned us, Jim Jones has sought to dope us, and southern conservatism has locked arms with white racism and founded a Moral Majority of distorted theology in the name of the Lord.

And yet, through it all, the church survives. Through it all, God's people are safe. Through it all, God's word endures. And if you don't understand why—the church is covered. The gates of hell cannot prevail against the church. The church is covered. The blood is on the doorpost. "A cloud covers the tent of the congregation, and the glory of the Lord fills the tabernacle."

But I brought this to your attention because this Word says "the glory of the Lord filled the tabernacle." I wanted to share this with you, for if there is to be a reversal of the fate and future of the church, if there is to be a moment when glory comes, I thought I ought to tell you that God dwells with those who prepare for Him. It is to the abiding credit of the children of Israel that they prepared a tabernacle. Yes, they were in a wilderness. Yes, they were plagued by poverty and haunted by doubt. Yes, they were caught in a swirling social order of idolatry and iniquity, but they did prepare a place for Him.

I'm led of the Lord to say at this moment that if there is no God-presence in your life, if there is no dimension of the divine in your life, the question is, have you prepared a place for Him? My Bible tells me God will not dwell in unclean temples. If you're looking for glory to come, it's time to say, "Search me and know my heart. Try me and know my thoughts." It's time to say, "Create in me a clean heart." Someone else said, "Search me, Lord. Shine a little light from heaven on my soul."

Not only that, but if you read this Word closely, it says that the tabernacle was there in the wilderness because the people had a willing spirit. Churches exist because of willing spirits. The black church has never been built because we had well-thought-out financial programs, the church is not built because we had sophisticated management systems, the church does not exist because we knew how to invest in stocks and bonds, the church is built because of soldiers of the cross who had a willing spirit.

It takes some consecrated pocketbooks to build the church. It takes some dedicated purses to build the church. It takes some men and women who are willing to bring their tithes and offerings to the storehouse, it takes those who are willing to bring the firstfruits of all their increase. Israel knew the presence of God in a fire by night and a cloud by day because they had a willing spirit. When the spirit gets right, a cloud of the presence of God will be manifest, and the glory of God will fill the tabernacle.

And so I keep on trying to understand the glory of God simply because, if I understand this word properly, it suggests that God chose to dwell among some strange people. The people to whom the glory of God was made manifest were not the best churchgoers you'd ever seen. These were the people who had given Moses a hard time. These were the church members that Moses had standing at the Red Sea with freedom in their grasp and liberty in their eyesight. These were the same folk that told Moses, "We should have died back in Egypt. We were doing all right with our flesh pots in Pharaoh's backyard. At least back in Egypt we had bread, and here we are out here and we're hungry. Back in Egypt we had a balanced budget because we had no budget."

These were they who were ex-slaves but who still had a slave mentality. These were the church members who were mumbling and grumbling and complaining and criticizing. But no matter how much you dislike the organization, no matter how opposed you are to the pastor, if God is in it, He'll work it out. If God is in it, He'll bless it. If God is in it, He'll work a miracle in the middle of a mess. God chose to reside among these recalcitrant, hard-headed, self-willed people. Not only did He reside, but He sent His cloud to cover the tent of the congregation, and the glory of the Lord filled the Tabernacle.

I'm still trying to understand what happens when glory comes. You see, my brothers and my sisters, there is something both awesome and awe-filled that occurs in the moment of worship. The Exodus record is silent on what went on in the context of their worship experience, but we do know that something occurred at tabernacle time.

I don't know about you, but I get concerned about some of the things we call worship. As I move about from church to church, I see a whole lot of worship that is contrived and conjured up. It's long on muscularity, but short on spirituality. Nobody loves worship more than I do. I believe what the Book says: "O worship the LORD in the beauty of holiness." I believe what it says: "Make a joyful noise unto the LORD." I believe what it says: "I was glad when they said unto me, let us go into the house of the LORD." I believe what it says: "Let everything that hath breath praise the LORD." But I don't care what you say, you can't manufacture the Holy Ghost. You can't force the Spirit by means of the mechanical. If you just worship Him "in spirit and in truth," He will come.

Sing the same hymns every Sunday, but He will come.

Pray the same prayer every Sunday, but He will come.

Preach the same gospel message, same people in the choir, same ushers at the door. You don't have to put on an outside show for an unfriendly world. He will come. Our foreparents had no organ, they had no PA system, no drums, no guitars, but you let somebody say, "Father, I stretch my hand to Thee," you let somebody say, "Amazing grace, how sweet the sound," He will come. And when He comes a cloud of contentment, a cloud of confidence, a cloud of sweet communion, a cloud of prevailing presence, a cloud of whispering hope, a cloud will cover the tent of the congregation and glory will fill the tabernacle.

The world still needs a church where God's glory is heard, seen, felt, and experienced. The fact of the matter is, the world needs the church. I know of no other institution so ordained by the omnipotence of God, so sustained by the omnipresence of God, so protected by the hand of God, so wrapped up in the will of God, and so saturated by the Spirit of God than the church.

The world needs the church where wounded souls can rest and troubled spirits pray.

The world needs the church where man and Maker can meet on solid ground.

The world needs the church where broken and bleeding bodies can touch the hem of His garment.

The world needs the church—"remove not the old landmark"—for I always want to be able to come back to my Father's praying ground.

The world needs the church, I tell you, but not just any church, not just four walls and a steeple. Not just any church, not a country club for the rich, not a sanctuary for pseudo-intellectuals, not a haven for the ne'er-do-well intelligentsia, not an exclusive club, but an inclusive fellowship.

The world needs the church, but a glorified church. A church where God gets the glory. A church where men are not ashamed to praise the Lord. A church where love leads the worship and peace prays the prayer and mercy minds the music and grace directs the choir and faith lifts the offering and the Holy Ghost is on preaching duty every Sunday morning.

The world needs a church where it's all right to say, "Amen"; it's all right to say, "Thank You, Jesus"; it's all right to get a little clapping in your hands and running in your feet. The world needs the kind of church where the cloud covers the congregation and the glory of the Lord fills the tabernacle.

There are some high and lifted moments of the religious experience which attest to the glory of God. God's glory is found in the context of worship. It was David who told us when glory comes, "The heavens declare the glory of God; and the firmament showeth his handiwork. Day unto day uttereth speech, and night unto night sheweth knowledge."

Not only that, but that same David said there was an antiphonal chorus that had a debate one day about the King of glory.

The basses asked the question, "Who is this King of glory?"

The tenors replied, "The Lord strong and mighty, the Lord mighty in battle."

The altos were not satisfied and they asked again, "Who is this King of glory?"

And the sopranos answered, "The LORD of hosts, he is the King of glory."

About that time, the conductor got weary of the conversation and said if you just want to know about Him, "Lift up your heads, O ye gates; and be ye lift up, ye everlasting doors; and the King of glory shall come in."

* * *

When glory comes. Isaiah said glory came for him one day when he saw also the Lord in the year that King Uzziah died. Isaiah said that it was there in the temple that an ordination service had been arranged. They called a council to ordain him that day. The Lord Himself preached the ordination sermon, and the power of His proclamation was so great the posts of the door moved and the house was filled with smoke. The council was composed of angels. Each had six wings. With two he covered his face, with two he covered his feet, and with twain he did fly. And while the ordination was taking place the council was going back and forth saying, "Holy, holy, holy, is the LORD of hosts: the whole earth is full of his glory."

And so today if you've never seen the glory of the Lord, don't worry about it, you shall. If you've never seen the cloud cover the congregation or the glory fill the tabernacle, you shall. If you've never seen the Holy Ghost take charge of the worship, you shall. Isaiah said:

> Every valley shall be exalted, and every mountain and hill shall be made low: and the crooked shall be made straight and the rough places plain: And the glory of the LORD shall be revealed, and all flesh shall see it together (Isaiah 40:4–5).

I want to see God's glory, and I want to see Him. John says we shall see Him one day when four and twenty elders shall gather 'round the celestial throne.

I want to see Him, my comfort, my joy, my peace, my pardon, my protection.

I want to see Him and look upon His face.

I want to "scale the utmost height and catch a gleam of glory bright."

I want to be able to say one day:

> Mine eyes have seen the glory
> Of the coming of the Lord,
> He is trampling out the vintage
> Where the grapes of wrath are stored;
> He hath loosed the fateful lightning
> Of His terrible, swift sword—
> His truth is marching on.
> Glory! glory, hallelujah!
> His truth is marching on.
>
> *Julia Ward Howe*

EPILOGUE

I was not prepared for what I saw. Our worship during these past two years had been held in a renovated gymnasium. The sanctuary we were to demolish seated in excess of one thousand. It was a common occurrence on any given Sunday to be filled to capacity, often including two overflow rooms equipped with closed-circuit television. On this Sunday, however, the press of the crowd was particularly heavy. Extra seats were brought in, officers gave up their front-row seats, associate preachers crowded the pulpit, and Metropolitan was alive and well. The atmosphere was electric.

This was the Sunday that representatives of our lending institutions were present. The architect and his staff crowded in, along with the general contractor and the supervisor of construction. Following the appropriate introductions, I gave the contractor the keys to the church, counseled him on the spiritual importance of the work, and offered the collective prayer of the congregation that the work would go safely and well, and that the church of our stormy dreams would finally rise from the ground broken for construction nearly three years before.

It may be appropriate to admit that "When Glory Comes!" raises many significant questions. (The questioning format is typical of my sermons.) The preacher caught in a storm has many such questions. It is not helpful, however, if the questions one raises are not adequately answered. Questions tend to build—and are deliberately designed to heighten—anticipation as well as participation. The hearer (or the reader) senses a letdown if the significance of the questions is not clearly revealed or if the answers are too simplistic. Even though the circumstance may "preach," it does not "teach"—kerygma without didache—a frequent trap for the preacher in a storm. The sermon must offer a "life vest" to those who come expecting a full and complete exposition of the Word.

There was deliberate intent in saying to those who had gathered that God, indeed, had been before us and behind us "all night long." The congregation had been through a very long night. How sweet to know that the dawn was breaking; what joy to realize that the storm was passing over!

"When Glory Comes!" was not prepared for the Metropolitan congregation. It was preached originally for the church of my childhood, the Mount Olivet Baptist Church of Columbus, Ohio, the church my father had served for more than three decades. I was confident that "the folks back home" were aware of the pain and struggle through which I had come; I had from time to time discussed with Dr. Charles Booth, the new pastor, the stormy predicament of my pastorate. I did not feel that I was a "prophet without honor," but I did feel compelled to say a word to those who were responsible for my spiritual tutelage that the storm had passed over and that, indeed, glory had come.

The force of the sermon was not to be felt, however, until nearly three weeks later when I preached it for the Metropolitan family. The worship was one of those moments kissed by heaven. It was, as it now seems, water to those who had for so long been trapped by desert lands without an oasis. Much in keeping with the textual word itself, "the glory of the Lord filled the tabernacle"! It was indeed a day of rejoicing—so rare, so sweet!

THE STORM IS PASSING OVER

Encourage my soul and let me journey on;
The night is dark and I am far from home.
Thanks be to God, the morning light appears;
The storm is passing over,
The storm is passing over,
The storm is passing over,
Hallelujah!

10

PREPARING FOR THE NEXT STORM

PROLOGUE

> Isn't it strange, the way certainty always comes before shattering?
> *Richard Bach*[1]

In the course of this book so far, I have tried to make several points about the storm in the contemporary church:

Every preacher is bound to encounter a storm sooner or later whether he knows it or not.

The preacher's storm is neither singular nor unique. Across the nation, the storm is a reality of life.

A wise preacher will learn to identify storm signals, will cultivate primary relationships, and will seek for himself a genuine friend.

Endurance may be more important than patience.

The storm passes over just when life appears gone.

There is yet another lesson, perhaps the most important, which the preacher-pastor must learn if he is to continue to preach through a storm. The lesson is simply this: *Another storm is coming!*

After the passage of a storm, it is tempting to bask in the thrill of victory. You suddenly have new friends: "Reverend, I was with you all the time." You gain new advisers: "Let's put our heads together and really run this show right!" Everyone congratulates you. It can go to your head. Enjoy it briefly— your humanity says you must—but never forget: *Another storm is coming!*

Shortly after my particular storm passed, I had a conference with a member of the congregation who had remained rather distant from the whole conflict. I asked him directly, "Do you think it's all over?"

His answer was cryptic but correct: "No!"

That particular storm had passed. But storms are always forming somewhere or other, and sooner or later another one will head your way.

Another storm is coming because it is a part of the Master's process of making men. When Jesus set His disciples in a boat to cross the always treacherous Sea of Galilee, it was not an unconscious or mindless decision on His part. The Master of those who are called to be "fishers of men" understood that there is a need for discipline in discipleship, and every seaman must be tested to be assured of his seaworthiness in later storms. How can a seaman advise others on the principles of storm survival if he has had no personal experience with storms in his own life? And one storm is not enough. Time and time again we must check our life preservers, examine our rafts for leaks, reexamine our spiritual navigational guidance equipment. The test is not a "simulation." It is not a "dress rehearsal." It is the real thing.

Another storm is coming.

There are other reasons for the coming of the next storm which must be examined with candor and precision. Another storm is coming because of the political nature of the church itself. The preacher who does not comprehend the political realities of church life is either a hopeless optimist or an incurable fool. The church is political. Its organizations, committees, boards, constitutions, and elections all serve to form the corpus of a political process which is as complicated and treacherous as the political party process currently afoot in our society. It is important that the pastor be aware of the political realities about him and seek to develop his own astute pastoral political guidance systems.

The apostle Paul stated quite clearly that "we wrestle not against flesh and blood, but against principalities, against powers, ... against spiritual wickedness in high places"

(Ephesians 6:12). There is, to be sure, "spiritual wickedness" in the church, and at base its orientation is political. It is the seed of the storm.

Prepare for the next storm because as long as there are cultural changes in the world around the church, the congregation will be affected by them. While we would want to believe that the church is separate from the world, the reality is that the church is dramatically and forcefully affected by the social dynamics of contemporary life. And wherever there is change, you have the possibility of a storm.

A storm can come in many forms. It may come in the form of resistance to change or of insistence on change. A storm may take the form of a violation, either conscious or unconscious, of time-honored biblical principles. More than a few storms will take the form of a challenge to the traditional position of pastoral authority within the congregation.

Congregations must also come to acknowledge and accept responsibility for their culpability in the storm-producing process. I began chapter 9 with a "job description" for the modern pastorate. If there is even a percentage point of accuracy in the description, "it is a grievous fault" and grievously shall we answer for it.

Preparing for the coming storm is the responsibility of both pastor and people. One cannot exist, in any sense of integrity and authenticity, without the other. The Rev. Hayward Wiggins of the Gethsemane Baptist Church of Houston, Texas, has rightly suggested that "the pastor is God's gift to the church; the church is God's gift to the pastor." One must nurture the other.

Especially in larger churches, pastors bear heavy administrative burdens, yet their congregations often insist that they also "serve tables" much in the manner described in Acts 6. Ministers who are required to "serve tables," to confine themselves to the niggling details of church life, to be "all things to all people" will, as did the original apostles, find themselves embroiled in controversy and conflict and storm. The church must return to the biblical model of seven men "filled with wisdom and the Holy Spirit" who are disciplined to aid the apostles (the size of the church boards has in far too many churches gotten completely out of hand). It must seek ways to "train the saints for the work of the ministry," thereby releasing the chosen and appointed apostles to give themselves "continually to prayer, and to the ministry of the word" (Acts 6:4).

It is certain that sooner or later another storm will come. When it does, there is one thing a preacher must not do. It may be tempting to follow the advice previously examined in the Book of Judges: "Put your hand over your mouth, come with us, and shut your mouth." Silence may seem like a way to avoid the storm or lessen its impact. It will do no such thing. In all probability, it will strengthen the force of the storm to an unprecedented level. No matter what the predicament of the preacher, he is always required, particularly in churches of the black tradition, to speak, to preach with power and with force. A failure to preach with power will only be a signal of weakness to adversaries and encourage them in their storm-developing process.

The question is not *if* a preacher should preach through a storm, but with what courage and determination and fearlessness shall he stand in John's shoes, somewhere between the living and the dead, and "preach the gospel in season and out."

"The Peril and the Power of Preaching" was given on the occasion of the installation of another of my sons in the gospel ministry. He had been called to serve a local congregation after working with me as assistant to the pastor for two years. He had been with me and shared with me through much of the storm I have previously described. The breathing-room-only congregation the evening of the ordination comprised not only members of the church to which he had been called but also a large contingent of persons from my own pastorate.

The sermon to be preached on that occasion had a three-pronged purpose. It was my purpose to simply remind this young preacher of the lessons he should have learned while with me as my "Timothy." It was my purpose as well to say a word to the congregation to which he had been called, a church which had only recently come through its own storm resulting in the dismissal of its pastor. It was my purpose, finally, to say a word to my own sheep as a shepherd who wanted them to know of my awareness of the peril, as well as my confidence, in the power of preaching. There shall be no need for an epilogue in this chapter. It will suffice to say that fire fell from heaven and glory filled our souls!

Sermon: THE PERIL AND THE POWER OF PREACHING

For which I am an ambassador in bonds: that therein I may speak boldly, as I ought to speak (Ephesians 6:20).

The Word of God, as it is expressed and codified in sacred Scripture, is insistent and persistent in its claim that there is no suitable substitute for the preaching of the gospel. Within the Testaments, both Old and New, God's Word is always carried on the fresh wind of a preacher preaching. The writers of the Old Testament may have been legalistic in their approach, historic in their world view, poetic in their perception or judgmental in their theology, but each in his own way was nothing more and nothing less than a preacher preaching.

The prophets of the ancient story were assigned the task of speaking to men on behalf of God and then speaking to God on behalf of men; the prophets were able to look backward through time to remind Israel of what God had done, stand in time to interpret what God was doing, and look through their prophetic telescopic lenses to see what God was about to do. Whether it was an Ezekiel crying in Chebar Valley Cemetery, Reverend Hosea hopelessly hooked on a whore, or Amos dusting off the leaves of a sycamore tree from the hills of Tekoa, the prophets were, at their base and at their zenith, preachers preaching.

If one were to look even to the pages of the New Testament and find there twelve dirty, undignified, uncultured, ignorant, and undisciplined disciples—whether your fondness is for James and John, the young fireballs, or for Matthew, the regenerated income tax extortioner, or for the unpredictable, impetuous, impious Peter—they were all, to a man, in the last analysis twelve preachers preaching. That is why I believe my claim is valid and my position is justified that there is, according to the Scripture, no suitable substitute for preaching.

Yet, if I were you, I would not be too hasty in the pursuit of the preaching profession. There is in the preaching process a certain charm; there is in the preaching moment an unmistakable presence of power; there is in the preaching position a certain aura which seems to boost the ego and which seems to inflate one's sense of self-importance; there is in the preaching personality an indefinable something which seems to cause some to see in us an appalling arrogance and yet is marked in some as a persuasive priestly piety; there is something in the preaching profession that gives new stature to the most common among us, gives new power to the weakest in the gathering, gives lucid tongues and facility of speech to those who used to stutter or stammer at every turn. There is, I tell you, an unmistakable persuasiveness and powerfulness and attractiveness and comeliness to the one who proclaims the Word in the pulpit. But if I were you I would not be too hasty in the pursuit of the preaching profession.

I thought I ought to give this word of caution primarily because as far as the claim and calling of the priestly profession are concerned, there is a strange mixture here of both peril and power. The contemporary proclaimer of the gospel is always living somewhere between burden and blessing. The proclaimer of the Word is always caught somewhere between the pain and the pleasure, the agony and the ecstasy. You may not believe me, you may not understand what I'm saying, but, brother pastor, you ought to know today that there is a peril in preaching.

* * *

Now the perilous nature of the preaching profession is nowhere more clearly to be seen than in Paul's letter to the church at Ephesus. The apostle Paul, as you know, wrote his letter to the Ephesian congregation somewhere around the year

A.D. 60, and his return address on the envelope was the Rome City Jail.

Paul, you remember, has argued his case before Festus and Agrippa and in a little storm-tossed boat that hardly made its way across the Adriatic Sea. Paul, the preacher, is now awaiting his own execution in the Roman Coliseum at the hand of Nero, who fashioned himself emperor of the then known world. In his letter, Preacher Paul gives timeless and time-honored advice to those who are engaged in and whose names are on the roll of the church of Jesus Christ.

Paul says to the church, whether you know it or not, you are engaged in Christian warfare, and that's why you need to "put on the whole armor of God." This battle, this warfare in which we are engaged, is not only spiritual, but has political connotations. "We wrestle not against flesh and blood, but against principalities, against powers, against the rulers of the darkness of this world, against spiritual wickedness in high places."

And then Paul says a word about the peril of preaching. Paul says, "Pray for me that I may open my mouth boldly to make known the mystery of the gospel for which I am an ambassador in bonds." Preacher Paul calls himself an ambassador in bonds. Paul, the only pastor most of these New Testament churches had ever known, defines himself as a prisoner in chains. Paul, the one who proclaimed that "all things work together for good"; Paul, the one who advised "nothing shall separate me from the love of Christ"; Paul, who set it down that "in Christ there is therefore now no condemnation"; Paul, who declared that "whosoever shall call upon the name of the Lord shall be saved"—this Paul has now come to the end of his journey, and he is not being consecrated bishop in the cathedral; he is not wearing the colorful robes of academic excellence; he is not exalted to some high rank of ecclesiastical stature; he is not installed as the pastor of Antioch Church where first they were called Christians. Paul says, "I'm in jail, I'm in prison, I'm in the hoosegow, I'm in the pokey, I am an ambassador in chains."

Let me pause here to say parenthetically that Paul had to

convince his readers that he knew who he was. The peril of most preachers is that they don't know who they are or what they are. The scourge of the Christian ministry today is that far too many of our brothers and sisters don't know who they are. They are unable to define themselves, suffering as it were from a ubiquitous identity crisis. The preacher is in peril who does not know who he is.

All through history men have struggled with the enigma of professional identity. Shakespeare's King Lear asked the question, "Who is it that can tell me whom I am?" René Descartes in 1637 was caught up on an ego trip when he declared, "*Cogito ergo sum.*" King Louis XIV told the seventeenth century that they could not exist without him when he said, "*L'état c'est moi.*" But Preacher Paul did not have any doubts about who he was or whose he was. I heard Paul say, "I know whom I have believed, and am persuaded that he is able to keep that which I have committed unto him" (2 Timothy 1:12). That's whose I am, and I know who I am. I am an ambassador in chains.

Well, if you know who you are, then I'm led of the Holy Ghost to tell you there are some perils in being a preacher. The first peril of the preacher is that *you will go to prison.* When you find yourself engaged in a life's work that you can't control, but it controls you, you're in prison. When you find yourself surrounded by people who don't understand why you do what you do, who hired you to do what you do and then won't let you do it, you're in prison. When you find yourself caught in an institution that calls a young man to bring about change in the church, and then the choir sings for its processional hymn "I Shall Not Be Moved," you're in prison. When you find yourself employed by people who call you to be the pastor, give you the title of "reverend," hang a sign on your door that says you're the pastor, hold an installation to give you the keys to the church, and then hold a church meeting to remind you that you ain't what they said you were, you're in prison. There is a peril in being a preacher because you will go to prison.

Paul says here, "I am an ambassador in chains." And I just

wanted to tell you that if you are in the chains of the preaching profession it means first of all that *you are not free.* Now there is a certain amount of freedom in the preaching and pastoral profession. Yes, you can come and go when you choose. Yes, you can convene the meeting and adjourn the meeting. Yes, you can give the call to worship and pronounce the benediction. But I'm here to tell you that you are not free. The church has voted to make you the pastor, but that only means they want you to be free to do what they want you to do.

But in another sense, let me remind you, you were called by a higher power. You are not free. You were consecrated by the hand of heaven. You are not free. You are commissioned to go by the apostolic urgency of the Holy Spirit. You are not free. You are to preach the preaching the Preacher bids you preach. You are not free and that, my brother, is the peril of preaching.

Paul said, "I am an ambassador in chains." And if you are in chains it means that *your integrity is vulnerable.* Everywhere you go, every step you take, somebody is watching to see if you mean what you say. Why do you think folk know your license plate number? They're not just playing the numbers. Somebody is watching you. They want to know where you go. That's chains. They want to know when you go. That's chains. They want to know what time you got back. That's chains.

Somebody is watching you, watching to make sure you're walking straighter than they are, watching so they can point a finger when you stumble and fall, watching so they can tell you a preacher is "just a man" like any other man, watching to be sure you are just a boy scout with his collar turned backward—mentally alert, physically fit, and morally straight. You are not free, and that means your integrity is vulnerable.

Well, Paul said, "I am an ambassador in chains," and that means the peril of preaching is that *you must live with the legacy of loneliness.* I would not frighten you today, but there is no lonelier man than the preacher. You will be lonely because you can't make friends with everyone. You show me a preacher who is buddy-buddy with everybody in his church and I'll show you a preacher who has lost his power. You can't be friends with all your deacons, you must be their pastor. You can't be chummy with all your trustees, you must be their pastor. You can't hang out until all hours of the night with the choir, you must be their pastor.

There's something that has to separate you from those whom you love. It alienates you from those you must lead. It divides you from those you must direct. It sets you apart from those whom you must guide. It's a lonely life. Paul didn't have many friends. He had to send for Timothy to bring his books and his coat. He said that his good friend Demas had forsaken him because he loved this present world. It's a lonely job. There is sometimes nobody—not mama, daddy, wife, children—nobody to count on. There's only one friend you can count on. "There's not a friend like the lowly Jesus, No not one!"

If you would be a preacher today I want to remind you that Paul said, "I am an ambassador in chains." Now, my brother, there is a difference between a diplomat and an ambassador. A diplomat is one who is sent for the purpose of negotiation. A diplomat is a professional compromiser. A diplomat is one who tries to soothe ruffled feathers and make everybody happy. Well, the pulpit is no place for a diplomat. Sometimes you have to say what folk don't want you to say. Sometimes you have to preach sermons folk don't want to hear. Sometimes you have to tell the truth when it hurts. You can't be a diplomat and be a preacher. Too many preachers now are slipping and sliding and trying to make wrong right, trying to make bad good. The pulpit is no place for a diplomat.

No, Paul said, "I am an ambassador." An ambassador is just a representative of the king. He doesn't have to apologize, compromise, or philosophize. All he has to do is say what the king tells him to say. Just be an ambassador on orders from the King. Just be an ambassador, an emissary of eternity. Just be an ambassador. The Bible is your portfolio. The Word of God is your message. The gospel is your news. The angels will carry your briefcase. The cherubim will announce your coming. The seraphim will protect you from hurt, harm, and danger. The archangels will bear you up lest you dash your foot against a stone. And if anybody asks you who you are, tell them you're God's man, tell them you're heaven's herald, tell them you're eternity's newsboy, tell them you are an ambassador for the King.

I thought I ought to tell you there is a peril in preaching, but—God bless your soul—there's also some power. Paul said he was an ambassador in chains, but if he could just get somebody to pray for him he'd have power to open his mouth boldly. If you open your mouth, God's got power for you.

He has power. God will be your "refuge and strength."

He has power. The eternal God will be your "refuge, and underneath are the everlasting arms."

He has power. "As many as received him, to them gave he power."

He has power. "Ye shall receive power, after that the Holy Ghost is come upon you."

He has power. "Even the youths shall faint and be weary, but they that wait upon the LORD shall renew their strength."

11

STORMS KEEP COMING

PROLOGUE

This Sunday was destined to be different. The cool, crisp air of that early December morning was washed by a silent, falling mist. On this day Metropolitan would enter her new church edifice.

I had been called to Metropolitan on the night of a great storm. I had, over the last seven years, experienced my own personal storm as well as the storm which engulfed and threatened the very life of the church. Now, on this day of days, the mist seemed like a reminder, the last lingering vestige of the storm.

I shall never forget that morning. I had risen early from my fretful sleep to pen the last lines of the sermon I was to deliver within a few short hours. My pen was still, but my mind raced. I was surrounded by members of my family who had come from across the country to share this hour with me. While they slept silently, I was alone with my private anguish and joy.

Images of all that had happened passed before me: the pain of my mother's death and the long-sought release from that deep distress . . . the ups and downs, the starts and stops in pursuit of this vision God had given me . . . the silent suffering of my wife and children, forced to bear a burden which was not of their choosing . . . the faithfulness of the people of Metropolitan who, through it all, would not be deterred or denied the fulfillment of this dream which had surely become their own.

As it happened, I was not alone. My wife had entered the room quietly just in time to wipe away the endless flood of tears which I could not explain or control. She did not need to say anything. Her presence was enough.

The hour had come. And a glorious hour it was. The Metropolitan sanctuary with seating for fourteen hundred was filled beyond capacity. People were standing around the walls. And yet it was not the beauty of the building or the press of the crowd or any of the other trappings of the moment. There was a strange and warm presence there which only the comatose or the dead could not sense or experience. And when that moment came and the congregation sang the Diadem—"All Hail the Power of Jesus' Name"—that peculiar presence engulfed our spirits and sent us on a flight of rapture we may never know again until we shall sing with a celestial choir.

We soared higher still as the choir sang,

> Jesus, you've brought me all of the way,
> You've carried my burdens all of the day.
> You're such a wonderful Savior,
> I've never known you to fail me yet.
> And you brought me, yes,
> You brought me all of the way.

The moment was electric. We knew then the vision had been fulfilled, the dream had become real.

Quite honestly I do not remember much of the sermon that morning. It was as though I was in it but not of it. I was the instrument to be used for God's purposes and His alone. I do remember the struggle which I had gone through to receive the word which He wanted to give for this hour. It had to be a time of rejoicing . . . but a time for sober reflection as well. It would be a time to celebrate our achievement as a Christian community . . . but also a time when God, through His Son Jesus Christ, should be magnified, and not the works of men.

Years before, I had shared with the Metropolitan family the words of Solomon as he prepared his people for the construction of the temple. As Solomon's words were fitting for the last sermon in the old Metropolitan, I was given to believe that his words would also be appropriate for the first sermon in the new Metropolitan.

So it was that in that majestic moment—when the storm had surely passed—I shared with them the words of Solomon upon the completion of the building of the house of the Lord, seeking simply to assure them of the promise of His presence.

Sermon: THE PROMISE OF HIS PRESENCE

In the ninth chapter of the First Book of Kings, these words are to be found:

> And it came to pass, when Solomon had finished the building of the house of the LORD and the king's house, and all Solomon's desire which he was pleased to do, That the LORD appeared to Solomon the second time, as he had appeared unto him at Gibeon. And the LORD said unto him, I have heard thy prayer and thy supplication, that thou hast made before me: I have hallowed this house, which thou hast built, to put my name there forever; and mine eyes and mine heart shall be there perpetually (vv. 1–3).

History will affirm and the ages will attest that it is unwise, ill-advised, and inexpedient to build a house for God and not be certain that God Himself has decided to be its resident. God's house is His house, and if it is His house and not our house, He alone must determine if this house is a suitable house in which He will dwell.

Perhaps you had not considered the options of God or the preferences of God or the prerogatives of God, but since we say it is His house, and since we say we built it for Him to serve Him, and since we say it is our offering and our sacrifice to Him, He must give to us a sign and a signal that He will accept it as His sanctuary and designate it as a habitation for the Holy. Just because we built the house does not give us the right to force it upon Him, press it upon Him, or require His residency within it. We must give Him the key, assign to Him both deed and title, divest ourselves of any options of ownership, abandon any proprietary claims we may think we have, and let Him decide for Himself if indeed this house will be His house. I am simply convinced today that it is unwise, ill-advised, and inexpedient to build a house for God and not be certain that God has decided to be its resident.

The urgency of my claim is framed and focused in an assurance that a church is not a church until God is present. A church is not a church unless and until God is resident within its walls and within its people.

> Without God the church is a ship without a rudder.

> Without God the church is a structure to be seen but no story to be told.

> Without God the church is a building with no one to believe in.

> Without God the church is a showpiece of ecclesiastical irrelevance and pietistic nonsense.

> Without God the church is a testimony to absurdity and a witness to foolishness.

> Without God the church is a museum of spiritual antiquities which possess neither sense nor substance.

> Without God, I tell you, the church is no more than a mere monument to "sounding brass and tinkling cymbal."

A church is not a church if God is not here.

> Men will pray, but there will be no power if He is not here.

> Gold-gilded organs may play, but there will be no sweetness in the notes if He is not here.

> Robed choirs may sing, but the music will not saturate the soul if He is not here.

> Tithes and offerings may abound, but "the windows of heaven" will not open up if He is not here.

> Preachers may proclaim the word, but souls will not be saved, sinners will not be converted, the lost will not be found, the blind will not see, the deaf will not hear, and the sick will not be healed if He is not here.

The church is only the church when there is an abiding confidence that here:

> Sin-sick souls can find Jeremiah's "Balm in Gilead."

Struggling spirits can find the higher ground of heaven's table land.

The forsaken and forgotten can find a friend, "all our sins and griefs to bear."

The disturbed and the distraught can escape the sinking, shifting sands of a crumbling culture and stand on solid rock.

The alienated and the frustrated can find a faith where there is nothing between the soul and the Savior.

The church is only the church where the insecure and the uncertain are able to find in this place a blessed assurance and a foretaste of heaven. But I assure you that the church is not the church if He is not here.

Because the presence of God is so critical and imperative and crucial to the existence of the church, and because the presence of God is so vital and necessary to the power and the permanence of the church, I wanted to share with you that which the Lord has revealed to me with regard to "the promise of His presence."

If you have a moment, I wanted to turn back the pages of history nine hundred years before the birth of Christ. Solomon, as you recall, was seated on the united throne of Israel. Solomon, by his own admission, had come to the throne when he was only a child. But somehow, through it all, God had blessed Solomon. Solomon's reservoirs were filled with gold and silver. His horses were counted by the thousands, his wives and concubines by the hundreds.

However, Solomon was not only blessed materially. Solomon, unlike his father David before him, was permitted to erect a temple for the living God. Solomon spared nothing in the building of the temple. His Phoenician ally, Hiram, provided craftsmen for the construction, designers, lumber, and gold. No doubt Solomon believed that nothing was too good for God and so the walls and floors were of gold. The cedars of Lebanon were transported for his use and even the throne and the attendant drinking vessels were made of ivory and gold as well.

We ought not overlook the fact that it took Solomon seven

years to erect the temple. Sometimes God has a way of delaying the building process until you build it the way He wants it built. I don't care what you say, God's time is not our time. He moves by His own method. He answers only to His own alarm clock. God still

> moves in a mysterious way
> His wonders to perform;
> He plants His footsteps on the sea
> And rides upon the storm.

It's hard to understand sometime, but His ways are not our ways, and His thoughts are not our thoughts. But then, that may be His way of saying, "If it's My house, I'll build it like I want to build it."

Now, the record says that when Solomon had finished building the house of the Lord, the Lord appeared to Solomon "the second time." When God has work for you to do, He not only appears one time, but a second time. And if I might offer a bit of parenthetical advice, my advice is, I wouldn't move out to build a house for the Lord in the first place if the Lord has not revealed it to you. I may as well be honest with you, if the Lord doesn't reveal Himself the first time, He will not be back for a second time. But when the Lord lays His hands on you, when the Lord reveals His work for you:

The first time He assigns you, but the second time He confirms you.

The first time He gives you sight, but the second time He gives you insight.

The first time He reveals His plan, but the second time He reveals His purpose.

When He appeared to Moses the first time, He said, "Put off thy shoes from off thy feet, for the place whereon thou standest is holy ground." But when He appeared to Moses the second time, He said, "Tell Pharaoh, let My people go."

The first time He appeared to Isaiah He showed him political power, kingly pomp, and regal pageantry. But the second time He appeared, Isaiah said, "In the year that King Uzziah died I saw also the Lord . . . high and lifted up."

198

The first time He appeared to Ezekiel all he could see was dry bones in a valley, and "Lo, they were very dry." But the second time He appeared to that graveyard preacher, all he could see was dry bones connecting one by one and a wheel in the middle of a wheel.

The first time He appeared to John, it was on an isle called Patmos and all he could see was the loneliness of isolation and the prison cell of solitary confinement. But the second time He appeared, John said he saw something else, "I saw a new heaven and a new earth . . . coming down . . . out of heaven . . . as a bride adorned for her husband."

The first time He appeared to Solomon at Gibeon Solomon asked for an understanding heart, but the second time the Lord appeared, He said, "Solomon, I have hallowed this house which you have built." And I just thought you ought to know, my brothers and my sisters, that if it is in God's will, God will appear for a second time.

And so, when He appeared to Solomon the second time, God said several things to him which had to do with the promise of His presence.

At the outset God said, "Solomon, I have heard your prayer and your supplication." I don't care what you say, whenever God's house is built, somebody has been praying. You can't build His house unless somebody knows the worth of prayer. I don't know if you know it or not, but somebody has been praying around here. Early Sunday morning, week in and week out, somebody's been praying around here. On Tuesday night, week in and week out, somebody's been praying around here. Way over in a midnight hour, somebody's been praying around here. When the darkness of the night came upon us and we didn't see sun, moon, or stars for many days, somebody's been praying around here. I don't know about you, but when I couldn't sleep at all and I tossed and turned all night long, I had a father praying down here and a mother pleading my case in glory.

Somebody's been praying around here. Somebody around here knew what it was to say, "Father, I stretch my hands to Thee, no other help I know."

But that's not all God said. Not only has He heard our prayer, but the revealed Word says, "I have hallowed this house which thou hast built." Now, my brothers and my sisters, this Word says, by obvious implication, that there's only so much that we can do. If He's going to live in it, if it's going to be His house, we can build it, but God has to bless it.

We can build it, but God has to put His benediction on it.

We can design it, but God has to dedicate it.

We can structure it, but God has to sanctify it.

We can plan it, but God has to purify it.

There's only so much that we can do.

The brick mason put it together with mortar, but God put it together with mercy.

The quarry provided the stones, but God is the Chief Cornerstone.

The contractor worked by blueprints, but God had a divine design.

The structure is welded steel, but the superstructure is the plan of salvation.

The engineer studied the strength of the structure, but the God we serve was here "before the hills in order stood" and long "before the earth received her frame."

The draftsmen said, "Build it on the rock foundation," but the Great Architect of the universe said, "Build it on the Word."

The architect wrote up the specifications, but God sent the architect a question:

Where were you when I unrolled the blueprints to the foundations of the earth?

Where were you when I hitched it to nothing and fastened it with my Word?

Where were you when I gave the wind its breath and taught it how to whistle when it cut around the corners?

Where were you when I shot the stars as a million skyrockets against the bosom of the black?

Where were you, Mr. Architect, when I scattered the fleecy white clouds against the bosom of the blue?

Where were you when I took a lump of clay and made man out of dust, stamped My image on his brow, put the quest of truth in his heart, and divinity in his soul?

Where were you, Mr. Contractor, when I laid the cornerstone?

Where were you when the morning stars sang together and the sons of God shouted for joy?

There's only so much we can do. It's God's house. If He's going to live in it, we can build it, but He has to bless it. That's why David said, "Except the LORD build the house, they labor in vain that build it: except the LORD keep the city, the watchman waketh but in vain."

Well now, my brothers and my sisters, as I come to my close I need to tell you that anything that belongs to you, if it's really and truly yours, you put your name on it. God told Solomon, "I have heard your prayer and I've hallowed your house, but I've done something else to let you know the promise of My presence. You don't have to worry, Solomon, I'll come in because I've put My name there. You can put a sign on the outside and call it what you want, but I've put My name there. Call it Metropolitan if you want, but don't forget I've put My name there."

And I might as well tell you it's not my name, and it's not your name. God's put His name there. His name is a sweet name. His name is lovely altogether. His name is music to my ears. His name is all my hope and all my trust.

*   *   *

I came to tell you that we have the promise of His presence. It's not a conditional promise, it's not a provisional promise, it's a perpetual promise. "I've put my name there, and mine eyes and my heart shall be there perpetually." He will be here.

If we stay on the Word and under the Cross, He will be here.

PREACHING THROUGH A STORM

Through storm and through rain, He will be here.

In the good times and in the bad, He will be here.

When the hosts of hell assail, He will be here.

When the winds blow and beat upon the house, He will be here.

When the death angel comes and bears some home, He will be here.

When we walk though the valley and the shadow of death, He will be here.

When high mountains get in our way, He will be here.

When deep valleys make us stumble and fall, He will be here.

When we're climbing up the rough side of the mountain, He will be here.

When men won't do right, He will be here.

When the heavens weep, the seas and rivers fill, He will be here.

When the thunder clears her throat in the heavens, He will be here.

When the lightning zigzags across the purple ether of the night, He will be here.

He will be with you:

> Teach all the nations My commands,
> I'm with you till the world shall end;
> All power is trusted in my hands:
> I can destroy, I will defend.

He will be with you. He told Joshua, "As I was with Moses, so I will be with you."

He will be with you. He told Isaiah, "When thou passest through the waters, I will be with thee; and through the rivers, they shall not overflow thee."

He will be with you. Jesus said, "Where two or three are gathered together in my name, there am I in the midst of them."

He will be with you, Jesus stood on a mountaintop one day and declared between time and eternity, "Go ye therefore into all the world . . . and lo, I am with you alway, even unto the end of the world."

He will be with you. How can you be sure, preacher? I'm sure
because

> I've seen the lightning flashing
> And heard the thunder roll,
> I've felt sin's breakers dashing,
> Which tried to conquer my soul;
> I've heard the voice of my Savior,
> He bid me still fight on—
> He promised never to leave me,
> Never to leave me alone.

INTERLUDE

It takes a while before mind and spirit can become
adjusted to any new environment. For many of us so closely
connected with this moment, the simple elegance and gran-
deur of the sanctuary was enough to take our breath away. And
it did. We almost became mute in the presence of this earthly
possession. We knew it was not ours, but there engulfed the
congregation a sense of holy pride in the victory, in the
achievement itself.

But I knew, as any preacher-pastor knows, that neither I
nor my people could afford to sustain the rapture of that
moment. We had to move on. We could not be so taken with
the building externals—wonderful as they are, they will one
day perish—that we failed to concentrate on the internals
which never pass away. We had to take up our work again.

Beyond all this, however, was my nagging confidence that
there would be other storms. If the building—the physical
structure—was no longer the focus of the storm, then what
would be? What more was there on the horizon of uncertainty
which would challenge and unsettle the people of God?

Storms are a part of the ebb and flow of life. They keep
coming, and we must be ready for them. That doesn't mean
that we should live in fear, always casting nervous glances
skyward for threatening clouds. But as we do the work of the
church—evangelism, missions, community outreach, the
gamut of Christian activity—there will be more than ample

opportunity for communication to break down, for goals and objectives to be misunderstood, for issues to develop on which members of the church will take sides. In short, there will be numerous opportunities for a new and perhaps even more violent storm to break out, and we must be ready.

Shortly before the new building was completed I had occasion to fly into Washington on a two-engine commuter plane. As we made our final descent, the small plane playing hopscotch among the clouds, I could see the patchwork plan of the nation's capital moving ever so slowly beneath. I recognized landmarks, the familiar buildings and monuments of this great city of the world. Unconsciously, it seemed, I began to pick out those places near where the church I served was located. The buildings seemed so small, the cars like ants crawling to a summer picnic, the stopping and starting of traffic like the changing of a computer screen before me. I wanted so much not only to see the church, but to see the spires of new steel coming out of the sacred ground over which we had struggled so long and with such pain. To my utter dismay, I could not see the church. So small was the structure, so minute the construction, that in the midst of the city which surrounded it, it could not be seen.

The airplane teaches such lessons. We are so caught up in our work on the ground that we lose the real perspective. We forget how small we are and how vast God is. It is not that our work is unimportant, but it must always be seen in the light of the reality which surrounds us. We must always remember the souls which are more important than cement. Only with the perspective of time and eternity can we answer the question, "How important are our storms, anyhow?"

Make no mistake about it. Storms are critically important. They are important for the health and wholeness of both pastor and people. The prophet-preacher must always warn the people of impending danger and point them to the source of ultimate salvation. In this connection, some two months after our entry into the new sanctuary, I lifted up a word of warning: "Storms Keep Coming!"

Sermon: STORMS KEEP COMING!

And when neither sun nor stars in many days appeared, and no small tempest lay on us, all hope that we should be saved was then taken away (Acts 27:20 KJV).

For many days neither sun nor stars appeared; the storm kept raging strongly, so that the last vestige of hope of our being saved was snatched away (Acts 27:20 MODERN LANGUAGE BIBLE).

It is not often that I give serious attention to the forecast of the weather. Generally, the weather will be what the weather will be. And, if the truth be known, in spite of what the predictions may be, there is absolutely nothing we can do to change the weather, no matter what the weather may be. I have discovered that if you don't like the weather today, just wait a little while, for if nature has its way, a change will surely come.

All of us are aware that weather prediction or weather forecasting is a precarious business at best. We can predict it, but we can't prevent it; we can prepare for it, but we cannot be certain of it; we can like it or dislike it, but we can't alter it, and we can't correct it; and that is why I say I give little serious attention to the forecast of the weather.

And yet, over the last few weeks, while I have not been engrossed in the weather forecasts, I have given considerable attention to weather patterns, and to the process by which weather forecasts are made. I've been learning and I've been listening to the weather prognosticators, and particularly so where there appears to be within the weather an element which is ominous and threatening and foreboding. Perhaps you have not given this matter much attention, but I have found it to be the case, that whenever a storm is coming the forecaster not only announces its predicted and projected arrival, but also tells the direction from which the storm is coming.

It may be that the storm was first detected in the balmy breezes of the South Pacific, and perhaps its path was tracked as it crossed the currents of the ocean and made its way across the uncharted pathways of the heavens, somewhere through the blue ether of eternity as it marched inexorably from west to east.

It may be that the storm was first seen blowing the hoary breath of Asiatic winds as it swept crisply over the snowy crests of the Canadian terrain and as it gained its strength while meandering through the icy and perilous peaks of Colorado's Rockies, certain of its destination from north to south.

Perhaps the storm found its form in some unseen yet ever present jet stream that gave to it the urgent persistence and precision to leave the barren and harvested fields of the Midwest and make its way to plant new snow caps on the hillsides of New Hampshire.

It may be that the storm knew its genesis in the gentle zephyr of Caribbean winds, or perhaps it was in the voice of Creation itself when nature opened her mouth and cleared its throat, spitting out tornadoes and twisters and hurricanes from the gaping Gulf of Mexico.

It is not often that I give serious attention to the weather forecast, but as I have watched and listened, and as I've watched the temperature move back and forth on her thermometer, and as I've seen the rising and falling of barometric pressure with every passing day, and as I've seen lightning flashing and heard thunder roll, of this one thing I am sure, that no matter from what point it starts—*storms keep coming!*

Now, it may well be that you will understand the meaning of this message when I tell you that in your life and in my life, storms keep coming. One would think, and perhaps one would hope, that when you have weathered one storm you wouldn't have to worry about facing any more storms. But, in fact, the reverse is true—*storms keep coming!*

If, in your life, you've had some financial storms, the ill winds of monetary adversity in your life have come, and it looks like the more you make the less you have to spend, and just as soon as you get that one bill paid you've been trying to get rid of for as long as you can remember, there's another one waiting in the mailbox—*storms keep coming!*

STORMS KEEP COMING

In your life you've had some physical storms. Perhaps you've been wrestling with some sickness for a long time. But just as soon as you get better and the doctor gives you a clean bill of health, something else breaks loose, some pain, some ache, arthritis stiffens your joints, and your blood pressure begins to rise and fall—something else breaks loose, I tell you, and you're sick all over again—*storms keep coming!*

In your life, and in my life, you've had some emotional upheaval when everything seems to be going backwards. Perhaps a divorce has disrupted your lifestyle. Perhaps tension has tightened the strings on your psychic health. Perhaps death has made a visit in the house where you live, and there's an aching void there that somehow cannot be filled, but just as soon as you come to contentment and peace, just as soon as you get your mind adjusted and your head screwed on right, something else will crop up just when you least expect it and turn your life upside down—*storms keep coming!*

In your life, and in my life, you've known some spiritual crisis. Your faith was shaken, your beliefs battered. Your soul's salvation was called into question, and somewhere along the line you lost the joy you once knew when first you found the Lord. But just as soon as you got your spirit right . . . just as soon as your soul began to get happy . . . just as soon as joy bells began to ring and you had a testimony to give, something happened that put your light out, and put water on your fire, and took the clapping out of your hands and the shouting out of your feet, and made you wonder what you come to church for anyhow. Storms! Storms! I tell you *storms keep coming!*

*   *   *

Quite naturally, then, this idea of the recurrence, the repetition, and the redundancy of the storm motif in our lives gave rise in my own mind to the question, "Why is it that storms keep coming?" Not only in their meteorological sense, but physically, emotionally, economically, socially, and psychologically—I'd like to know why do storms keep coming?

Perhaps there are some lessons in the storms that we are not seeing.

Perhaps there is some meaning, some significance in these internal and external disturbances we're not properly appropriating.

Perhaps there is some insight to be gained, some perspective to be sharpened with which we are not in tune. And that's the reason I'd like to ask today, why is it that the storms keep on coming?

And so, permit, if you will, a personal perspective on this storm situation. It may be, in the first instance, that *my grandfather was right!*

You did not know William Hicks. You never heard my grandfather's gentle voice or saw his captivating smile. You never saw him walk, preacher that he was, with his precisioned step and sure gait. I wish you had known him, as I did, in his last years when the chisel of time had etched out furrows of faith on his brow and when his frail hands guided me to his bedside to teach lessons that time cannot erase. But Granddaddy had something to say about storms.

Whenever the skies would darken on the horizon, and whenever the thunder would roll out her bass drum and beat out her unpredictable rhythm as the pelting rain made of the roof an echo chamber, and whenever the lightning would strut its stuff in a zigzag performance before the curtain of creation, Granddaddy would say, "Little Henry, sit down now. That's God talking!"

I believe Granddaddy was right. When the storms of life come upon us, God is talking.

When the storms in our home come upon us, God is talking.

When the storms in our personality come upon us, God is talking.

When the storms in our church come upon us, God is talking.

We may not understand His language.

We may not comprehend His chosen idiomatic expression.

We may not like to hear the tone of His voice.

But when the storm comes, God is talking. Don't you know that

> He who is in charge of the sunshine is also superintendent of the shadows?
>
> He who works with the wind also regiments the rain?
>
> He who sends the snows of winter also ushers in the flowers of spring?

But God's job is to take charge of the storm, and our job is to listen to the lesson He teaches by the storm. Sometimes He doesn't say much, but if you listen, in the midst of the storm there will be "a still, small voice" and all it says is, "Be still and know that I am God: I will be exalted among the heathen, I will be exalted in the earth" (Psalm 46:10). When the storm comes, God is talking. And that's why I keep on telling you, *storms keep coming.*

But while I'm on this journey, permit me, if you will, a biblical perspective. Perhaps there is, couched deeply within the Word of God, an explanation or an understanding of the repetitive nature of life's storms. No doubt . . .

Noah knows something about storms. God sent a storm one day. It was not a little storm but a big storm. The storm was so big, in fact, that they tell me it rained forty days and forty nights. So devastating and destructive was the force of the storm that only the animals could get on board two by two. What did you learn, Noah? I heard Noah say, "I learned some lessons about these storms. God gave me a rainbow sign. There'll be no more water, it's the fire next time."

Jonah knows something about storms. Jonah didn't expect a storm that day when he left the port of Joppa on a luxury liner bound for distant Tarshish. There were blue skies and a cloudless horizon when he left, but he wound up in the belly of a whale before he got where he was going. Jonah, you had a storm that night. What did you learn, Jonah? What I learned was, "You can run, but you can't hide!"

Peter knows something about storms. Peter saw Jesus one

night walking on the Sea of Galilee. And you know what he said was, "Lord, if it be thou, bid me come unto thee on the water." But the Book says the winds were contrary. The waves got frisky and Peter lost his footing. Peter, what did you learn from the storm? What I learned was, "If you want to keep your balance in the midst of the storm, if you want to maintain your equilibrium in the midst of the storm, keep your eye on Jesus!"

Those two builders knew something about storms. They both built their own houses. No doubt they both had the finest materials and no doubt they used the latest architectural designs. But after a while they tell me a storm rose up. The rains came, the winds blew and beat upon those houses. Nobody has seen the man who built his house on the sand, but maybe the other builder with the house that survived the storm, maybe he can tell us. What did you learn, Mr. Successful Builder? What did you learn, Mr. Wise Contractor? What I learned is, "If you want to have a house that can survive the storm, you have to build your hopes on things eternal and hold to God's unchanging hand."

My Bible teaches some lessons on storms, but I still have to tell you today that storms keep on coming!

Well, if you have the time today, I wanted to look a little closer at this storm situation. Since the storms keep coming, maybe we might want to find out how to handle the storms. And it occurs to me that if you want to know how to handle a storm, you ought to talk to some folk who've been in the storm. If you think your boat is about to sink, you ought to discuss the matter with some seamen who know what storms are all about. When I see young people in the church and those who are just beginning their voyage on the sea of life, I'd recommend that you talk with some of those older veterans of the sea who've been here longer than you have.

You think you've got some storms, but there are some folk who didn't just get here yesterday, and they know what it means to say, "I been in the storm so long." I know you don't talk very much with your mothers and fathers, and I know you don't confer too often with your grandfathers and grand-mothers, but they can tell you about the storms.

Too often young folk have given up on themselves and given up on others and given up on the church as a realistic guide for their lives because the storms keep on coming. And I don't mean to be presumptuous or to put words in anybody's mouth, but if you talk with some of these old sailors, they'll tell you that when the storm rages, when the rain comes, when the wind blows, when enemies assail you, when foes come upon you, when dark clouds gather round you, whatever you do, stay on the boat!

Don't quit in the storm. Stay on the boat.

Don't give up in the storm. Stay on the boat.

Don't jump overboard with the first wind that slaps you in the face. Stay on the boat.

Don't abandon your life vest, don't lower your sail, don't cut off your engines, and don't participate in the mutiny of self-destruction. Stay on the boat.

It's an old ship, a leaky ship, a weatherworn ship, but it's a good ship. Somebody said it's the Old Ship of Zion, but it's landed many a thousand. All you need to do is get on board and then stay on board because *the storms keep coming.*

*   *   *

Well, I've got to go now, but as I'm on my way, I wanted to take a look at a preacher named Paul who is, by his own admission, a veteran of the sea. Maybe Paul can tell us what to do about these storms that keep on coming. I've been reading this Word, and it says that Paul was a prisoner bound for a final time for Rome to stand trial. By his account Paul left Palestine somewhere in late August or early September. Paul sailed to the east and north of Cyprus to Myra on the southern coast of Asia Minor. In Myra they changed ships and barely made it to Fair Havens on the southern coasts of Crete. It was on this last leg of the journey that Paul discovered once again in his own life that, indeed, *storms keep coming.*

The Book says that while they were traveling, a storm rose

in the sea. They did everything they knew how to do, but they were up against a storm, a tempestuous wind, and they called it "Euroclydon."

> They couldn't guide the ship, so they let it go, and the storms kept coming.
>
> They undergirded the ship and pulled down the sails, but the storms kept coming.
>
> They went down in the cargo bay and started tossing cargo overboard, but no matter, the storms kept coming.
>
> They took the tackle of the ship and threw it overboard, but the storms kept coming.
>
> They had been in the storm for fourteen days—no sun to brighten their days, and no stars to guide them by night—and the storms kept coming.
>
> They gave up all hope of being saved, and the captain and the crew began to say their final farewells!

Listen to Paul: "While you fellows were fighting the storm and struggling with the sea, I've been down in my cabin holding prayer meeting. I came to tell you to be of good cheer, for there stood by me this night the angel of God, whose I am and whom I serve."

I talked to the angel last night. I told the angel:

> "When the storms of life are raging, stand by me.
> When the storms of life are raging, stand by me.
> When the world is tossing me like a ship upon the sea,
> Thou who rulest wind and water, stand by me!"

Paul said that when the storms kept coming they cast their anchors and waited for the day. My brothers and my sisters, when the storms keep coming, your survival is not in your sail, it's in your anchor.

And I came to tell you today:

> If the storms don't cease
> and if the winds keep on blowing in my life,
> my soul's been anchored in the Lord!

EPILOGUE

A Time for Serious Preaching

The primary question with which this work began has yet to be answered. Essentially the question is whether or not the preacher who is caught in a storm within the church can effectively preach to and through the storm. Is the proclamation of the gospel of Jesus Christ still a viable tool for the easing of tension, and is one person with one mindset preaching to hundreds of persons with a multiplicity of mindsets sufficient to bring about a genuine ministry of reconciliation?

On the face of it, it seems ludicrous. Perhaps we expect too much of the preaching event. Isn't there some other resource preachers could use? Isn't there some other skill which would be more productive in storm-settings which preachers have yet to learn? Wouldn't our time be better spent seeking a new approach to preaching which might replace this outworn and perhaps outdated method of priestly persuasion? Isn't there some new mode of ministry management which we have overlooked?

The answer to all these inquiries is a resounding no! In my opinion, preaching is still the primary and most viable tool which has been given for our benefit and use. At times preaching may seem a fragile instrument, unequal to the task, but the apostle Paul, speaking to the Corinthian Christians, counsels us wisely, "For the preaching of the cross is to them that perish foolishness; but unto us which are saved, it is the power of God. . . . It pleased God by the foolishness of preaching to save them that believe" (I Corinthians 1:18, 21). The preacher-pastor can and must preach to and through the storm. If there be no preaching, then both preacher and church, I fear, will perish in the storm.

It is clear that preachers and preaching are facing difficult days. It is precisely because the days are difficult and the storm so violent that now, more than ever, in the words of Henry H. Mitchell, dean of the Virginia Union School of Religion, there

must be a "recovery of preaching."[1] I am thoroughly convinced that preaching is still that medium of divine-human
communication through which God makes His will known to
men and ultimately to His church.

If we abandon preaching and our voices are hushed, who
shall speak a word to this generation? Shall we simply agree as
one to declare that indeed there is no word from the Lord?
Certainly not. Our storms are not to be compared to those of
preachers in years gone by.

"Storms?" Martin Luther asks. "What storm?"

"Storms?" Wycliff, Zwingli, and Hus ask. "What storm?"

"Storms?" Martin Luther King, Jr., asks. "What storm?"

"Storms?" my slave ancestors who built the church as we know
it from brush arbors and shanties and lean-tos, who memorized
Scriptures they could not read and sang hymns for which they
had no music and no hymnbook, ask. "What storm?"

These examples from history are instructive to this
purpose. It is not that these saints were oblivious to storms—
which they surely faced head-on—but that they found a way
to live through them, thereby redirecting history through their
ministry. More to the point, in light of the storms which they
faced, our own storms seem to pale in significance.

The storm provides an appropriate setting in which one
can surely preach—with integrity, with an authentic voice,
with prophetic urgency—and the preacher must be willing,
with Paul, to "cast four anchors" and preach until the storms
shall cease.

I say again that the preacher-pastor must preach in a
storm. And essentially so because preaching still produces
converts to the cause and to the kingdom. The church to which
any preacher is called is primarily composed of those who are
found there. If, however, the church is committed to the
mission of claiming men and women for Christ, the composition of that congregation will of necessity be altered. As
persons are born into the church as well as through the great
priestly acts of the church, baptism, infant dedication, and the

like, a change will surely come in the composition and character of that congregation, a change that comes only through the urgent preaching of the Word of God.

If the preacher does not preach through the storm, what options are then left? Precisely none. There are times, admittedly, when the preacher will want to do anything but preach. There will be those moments of such spiritual barrenness and drought, those endless Saturday nights when the preacher can find nothing to say, much less the will to say it. There will be those Sundays when the preacher fairly staggers to the pulpit knowing that rather than preach he needs to be preached to. Yet, this is precisely the moment, if one will make oneself available, that God can use both preacher and people to His purposes. In every sermon there is therapy—and there ought be—for both pulpit and pew. There are no other options, there is no escape. The authentic preacher must preach through the storm.

I come to this conclusion because I believe that this is a time for serious preaching. Serious preaching, as opposed to non-serious preaching, is thoroughly committed to the prophetic tradition in which we stand and is willing, at all costs, to pronounce the demands and the rewards of the gospel of Jesus Christ. The times in which we preach—socially, politically, morally, economically—are indeed serious. Unfortunately, the state of religion in America today has fostered an era which has spawned everything from Jim Jones fanaticism to the right wing reactionism of the ilk of the Moral Majority.

Nevertheless, I believe this is a great time, a great opportunity, for the church and for those who proclaim its gospel. We are living in an era of church growth, when people from all walks of life are turning to the church in unprecedented numbers, and responsible religionists have a mandate to insure and assure that what they hear and what they are taught is serious in both content and form. I have found that there yet remains in the churches an excitement that surrounds the preaching moment. As the preacher mounts the pulpit there is, and there should be, a kind of holy tension and an urgent expectancy that a Word from the Lord is soon to be heard. Preaching is still an awe-filled moment and an awesome responsibility.

Moreover, serious preaching is demanded in spite of and because of the storms we face. The gospel of Jesus Christ still contains serious solutions both for pulpit and for pew. How important is this process we call preaching! Is it possible that we can be so caught up in our petty church fights and squabbles that we fail to attend to the great watchwords of our faith? The gospel of the saving grace of Jesus Christ is too important to be made small or trivial or of no effect.

What we have to say may not be couched in the king's finest English, it may not be philosophically profound or even reflective of great theological thought. But the gospel was not necessarily meant to be profound. It is designed through its simplicity to speak to the deep issues of life. We handle holy words which by their very nature speak to us and to our storms: hope, faith, love, redemption, justification, grace . . . amazing grace! These are the watchwords of the watchman. These are serious words for serious preachers.

Ultimately, preachers who do not preach a serious gospel will not be taken seriously. Preaching is not a sideline, it is not an avocation, it is not a hobby. It is the very umbilical cord, the lifeline, which links the preacher with the One who bids him preach. The congregations to whom we preach must understand that the preaching event is not a question of "shall I?" Rather, it is the imperative of "I must!" This preaching business is not a part-time venture, and the preacher remains ever on call. Who knows but that in some midnight hour an urgent call might go forth to come with a healing hand and with a praying spirit? But such a serious call will only come to serious preachers. This is a time for serious preaching.

If I Had to Do It Over Again

The question is often asked, "What would you do if you could live your life over again?" At this juncture the reader might well ask, "What would I do differently if I had to live this particular storm over again?" Are there some concepts or principles which should be passed on to those who are soon to enter the pastorate and subsequently their own storms? What counsel or advice do I, a sea-tossed preacher, have to give?

If I had to do it over again, I would find myself *preaching more on the great love themes of the Bible.* To be sure, when caught in the throes of a storm the preacher will not be given to many thoughts of love. And yet, if there is a biblical theme which cries out to be preached, it is the theme of love. To know that God loves us even as we struggle to love and to forgive each other is the essence, the heart, of the Good News. Rather than attack with sermons, a more positive note must be sounded, a more positive theme expounded, no matter how difficult the task.

If I had to do it over again, I would try to follow the New Testament injunction and "*tell it to the church.*" Many members of our congregations do not come to the preacher's aid simply because they do not know the nature and the scope of the problem as he perceives it. In the storm there is, I believe, a natural inclination to turn inward and thus to take a posture of silent strength. The church, however, cannot be responsive to the minister's needs, either personal or professional, if he does not freely share with them that which in his opinion has caused or created the storm.

I would also seek to communicate with the congregation orally as opposed to using the written word. The reports, the newsletters, the pastoral letters sent by mail to the congregation are fine in their place. They will not substitute, however, for the shepherd who speaks directly and honestly to his sheep. The late Dr. Sandy F. Ray of Brooklyn, New York, constantly warned preachers of putting too much on the printed page. As he put it, the people will pay more attention to the paper than they will to the pastor. There can be no support for that which is not understood. Until the pastor speaks, the congregation is left to the ravages of grapevine rumor and suspicion. When the storm rages, the preacher must speak up to be heard.

If I had to do it over again, I would *ask more questions and give fewer answers.* The other side of the coin mentioned above is that it is possible for the preacher-pastor caught in a storm to talk too much. If he is always placed in the position of being the target, of being on the defensive, he will be hopelessly lost in a swirling sea.

There is sage counsel in listening more and talking less so that when you do speak, it will be a word of unmistakable clarity and will be more decisive in its effect. The preacher who is able to ask the right question at the right time can take the wind out of many storms before they begin.

If I had to do it over again, I would *surround myself with allies whose integrity and commitment to Jesus Christ is beyond question.* There are some who would suggest that when you are caught in a storm, when adversaries are all around, take that adversary and bring him or her closer to you so you'll know what they are doing and thinking and thereby eliminate the prospect of surprise. I say, again, there is no redeeming value in making the same mistake twice. The work to which we are called and committed is serious. Those who are around us at the decision-making level must be committed to the principles of Jesus Christ, and they must also be a part of that core of persons who will work tirelessly to guide the church along the path which the pastor and the congregation have determined.

This is not to suggest that leaders should be mindless. It is to say that the preacher whom the church has called to be its temporal leader must be given every opportunity and resource to achieve the highest good. The church which does not insist upon this kind of dedicated and consecrated leadership destroys the integrity of its work and will ultimately see the destruction of its ministry.

If I had to do it over again, I would *combine a program of evangelism with the building program.* The church is fooling itself to believe that it can have program or power divorced from people. If the storm is not occasioned by a building program, then whatever the goal may be can be achieved simply by "bringing them in." I don't know how many times I have been told, "Reverend, your program will really be on track as soon as you have a few more funerals!" I have discovered, however, that those who most seriously oppose the pastor or his program do not die. And if they die, they leave scads of children!

The church which one ultimately leads is one that comes to the congregation through the preaching of the gospel and through a consistent program of evangelism and outreach. The wheat and the tare must grow together, to be sure. The weeds, however, will take care of themselves. It is the preacher's responsibility to grow more wheat. Such growth comes along through the preaching and teaching of the Word.

If I had to do it over again, I would *give more time to sermon preparation and personal spiritual development.* The person the preacher is most likely to seriously neglect in any storm situation is the preacher himself. Neglect is born of a kind of "the-captain must go down with-the-ship" mentality.

Nothing could be further from the truth. A Spirit-fed and Spirit-filled mind is an absolute essential if responsible and serious preaching is to take place in the storm situation. The committees, the boards, the programs, the strategy sessions have a way of consuming an inordinate amount of the preacher's time and energy. But these things are not the primary claim of our calling, nor are they critical to the development of a strong spiritual base for the church. This is the process of "serving tables" against which Acts 6 specifically warns. Personal spiritual development is critical if we do not want to be guilty of being so busy saving others, as Paul has suggested, that we fail to save ourselves.

This spiritual development of which I speak tends toward the lessening of the fear which the preacher brings to the storm. The storm, viewed properly, may well be the preacher's ally and not his adversary. Marcus Dodd is reported to have said that the wind blows where it will, but experienced sailors know where the trade winds blow and then put themselves into the way of it.

Ultimately, if I had to do it over again, I would *continually assure my people of my love for them.* The storm affects both pastor and people. During those times of storm the congregation must be assured of the steadfast love and affection of the one they have called to serve them. Kindness, empathy, and grace under pressure will do more to bind up the church than any other strategy known to man. He who preaches the word of love which fell from the lips of the One who is love must find that love expressed most clearly in his actions and deeds. Such an abundant and genuine outpouring of love will permit the preacher to preach through and to the storm. Paul is right, "Love never fails."

Speak the Truth in Love

By even casual observation one will detect that the Metropolitan Church of those storm-filled years has been dramatically and, I believe, unalterably changed. Oddly enough, the building alone is not responsible for that change. The external structure is really but a shallow and superficial image of the profound change which has clearly taken place. There is a spiritual beauty which has reshaped the countenance of this part of the body of Christ. Once again, as in former years, the church has become a center of community activity; Bible study abounds; new commitments to Christ are being made at unprecedented levels; internal organizational activity flourishes; a genuine sense of harmony and unity has returned and now characterizes the board structure; there is, to be sure, an unmistakable joy that marks our worship. More than this, however, there is an at-ease-ness, a tensionless, more open, and productive relationship between pastor and people—based, I believe, on mutual trust and love. We, pastor and people, have weathered the storm together and we are stronger because of it.

On balance, however, one must never arrogantly assume or presume that this fair weather will be the perpetual forecast. It cannot and will not be so. After all, storms are an inescapable reality in the seasons of life. But at this point, the collective church has a common experience/knowledge base by which to govern and to judge its actions in future storms.

There has been, to be sure, an element of honest and candid boldness to this work. That one should speak so openly and freely and publicly to this issue of internal conflict and storm fairly boggles the mind. I am convinced, however, that we need not be ashamed of conflict—the shame of it all would be to fail to understand it, to fail to place it in a spiritual-biblical context, to fail to profit by it and to fail to share with other pastors and churches the lessons which the storm so generously taught.

Indeed, this entire work is written as the writer believes the people have granted the right for this preacher to "speak the truth in love." The unfolding years shall reveal if this judgment is confirmed. Only love can endure; only love can bring pastor and people safely home to harbor. Love, tender in its toughness, will ultimately prevail in any wind. Without that love, seamen will surely perish.

A Word From the Captain of the Ship

The journey through this storm has been long, the struggle has been demanding, and the ultimate spiritual cost inestimable. I am confident, however, that Metropolitan—and any church with similar stormlike situations—will be a stronger and more viable church because of it. There is nothing to match the sweetness of the air on the morning after the atmosphere has been washed by nature's storms. In like manner, there is nothing to be compared with the sweet fellowship and the odor of genuine joy which will engulf a church after its storm experience. Nevertheless, it is natural and inevitable that the preacher and the people who experience such a storm will often wonder aloud if they will ever know that refreshing sweetness.

To know that sweetness, every preacher-pastor must acknowledge that he is not the captain of the ship. The preacher can only, at best, be known as first officer. The guidance of the ship is left in surer, safer hands than ours.

To know that after-storm sweetness, the preacher-pastor must be patient with his people as well as with himself. Both are in the stage of learning, the stage of becoming. What appears to be of urgent moment today may not seem so when viewed from the balcony of some unknown tomorrow.

To know that sweetness, one must be willing to trust implicitly in the Captain who not only guides the ship, but who is in control of the water and the storms. The Old Ship of Zion has landed many a thousand. It will, I am sure, land for you one day and for me, I know, as well.

God be praised for the Captain of the Ship, who does not speak in unknown tongues or foreign dialects, but in our native tongue declares, "Lo, I am with you always, even to the end of the world."

> Though the world that I've been living in
>   collapses at my feet
> And when life is shattered and torn,
> Tho' I'm windswept and battered,
> I can cling to His cross
> And find peace in the midst of the storm.
>
> There is peace in the midst of a storm-tossed life;
> There's an anchor, there's a rock to build my faith upon;
> Jesus guides my vessel, so I'll feel no alarm,
> He gives me peace in the midst of the storm.
>
> *Unknown*

NOTES

INTRODUCTION

1. Jeffrey K. Hadden, *The Gathering Storm in the Churches* (Garden City, N.J.: Doubleday, 1969), 32.

CHAPTER 1

1. *Macbeth*, act 5, sc. 5, lines 22–28.

CHAPTER 2

1. Richard Bach, *The Bridge Across Forever* (New York: William Morrow, 1984), 68.

2. Gene E. Bartlett, *Postscript to Preaching* (Valley Forge: Judson, 1981), 34.

3. Carnegie Samuel Calian, *Today's Pastor in Tomorrow's World* (New York: Hawthorn, 1977).

CHAPTER 3

1. H. Beecher Hicks, Jr., *Images of the Black Preacher: The Man Nobody Knows* (Valley Forge: Judson, 1977).

2. Norman Cousins, *Human Options* (New York: W. W. Norton, 1981), 52.

3. Gene E. Bartlett, *The Audacity of Preaching* (New York: Harper, 1962), 146.

CHAPTER 5

1. Cousins, *Human Options*, 39.

2. M. Scott Peck, *People of the Lie* (New York: Simon & Schuster, 1983), 76n.

3. Ibid., 74.

4. Cousins, *Human Options*, 61.

74971

5. Peck, *People of the Lie*, 71.

CHAPTER 7

1. Sandy F. Ray, *Journeying Through a Jungle* (Nashville: Broadman, 1979), 96.

2. Richard Bach, *Bridge Across Forever* (New York: William Morrow, 1984), 86f.

CHAPTER 8

1. John Claypool, *Glad Reunion* (Waco, Tex.: Word, 1985), 106.

CHAPTER 9

1. Edward Bratcher, *The Walk-on-Water Syndrome* (Waco, Tex.: Word, 1984), 205.

2. Ibid.

3. Ibid.

CHAPTER 10

1. Bach, *Bridge Across Forever*, 139.

CHAPTER 11

1. Henry H. Mitchell, *The Recovery of Preaching* (New York: Harper & Row, 1977).